PERSONAL FINANCE FOR TEENAGERS

The Fast Track to Financial Literacy with Teen-Tailored Money Management Skills - Hands-On Activities for Earning, Saving, Budgeting, Spending, and Investing

Ben Clardy

Contents

Introduction

Being a teenager in today's world is challenging. You've got peer pressure nipping at your heels, trendy temptations lurking around every corner, and a school system that thinks teaching you about money is about as important as learning to whistle underwater.

Reading, writing, math, science, history—they're all pieces of a larger puzzle that help shape your understanding of the world around you. But here's the thing...

...*there's a piece missing*.

Without this critical piece, you're at a disadvantage. You're thrust into a money-driven world that plays by specific rules, but without the missing piece—you have no idea what the rules are.

The missing puzzle piece?

Personal Finance.

Introduction

You could be the most brilliant mathematician or the most well-paid professional athlete, but if you can't manage your finances, you'll always be struggling to make ends meet.

This book comes in where school left you hanging. It's designed to take you from piggybank to portfolio, from allowance to abundance, and from FOMO to financial freedom.

In this book, we'll tackle a wide range of essential money topics. Most will be immediately applicable to your life as a teen, while a few are more advanced concepts that you'll encounter once you're a young adult.

Why cover these future topics now? Because understanding them early on will help you make smarter decisions today that'll set you up for success tomorrow. Think of it as a roadmap for your financial journey—both the path you're on now and the one that lies just over the horizon.

We'll tackle essential money topics that every teen should know:

- Learning valuable side hustle skills (*so you can buy stuff without asking for an advance on your allowance*)
- How to maintain a budget (*so that the foundation of your food pyramid is not constructed of ramen*)
- The art of saying "no" to peer pressure (*without losing your friends*)
- Why investing isn't just for older people and Wall Street pros (*because you're never too young to start building your financial empire*)
- How to deal with student loan debt (*without the*

temptation to fake your own death and survive on a remote island)
- Navigating the treacherous waters of credit cards (*without drowning in a sea of debt and regret*)
- The importance of emergency funds (*because life has a funny way of throwing curveballs when you least expect it*)

So, are you ready to take the next step?

I hope so, because this isn't just another boring book about numbers — it's your golden ticket to a future filled with prosperity, freedom, and endless possibilities.

But, before you go any further there's something to consider...

<u>The chapters that follow will change you</u>.

You'll know things that most people can't comprehend.

You'll speak a language that most people don't understand.

You'll have opportunities that most people are blind to.

Once you turn this page, your transformation will begin.

Can you handle that?

If not — simply close this book and go about your life.

If so — *turn the page and let's find that missing puzzle piece.*

Chapter 1
The Basics Of Money

Money is not everything...
...but it ranks right up there with oxygen.
—Zig Ziglar

Money. It's a concept that touches every aspect of our lives, from the daily necessities we buy to the long-term dreams we save for. But how much do you really know about this powerful force that shapes our world?

The History Of Money

Money is so much more than colorful pieces of paper we exchange for goods and services. It's a reflection of human civilization itself. It's a tale of ingenuity, advancement, and necessity that has shaped our world in ways we often overlook. By the end of this chapter, you might just find yourself looking at those bills in your wallet with a newfound appreciation for the history they carry.

Bartering

Picture this: you're a young farmer in ancient Mesopotamia, and you've got a bunch of goats that are the envy of the village. Your neighbor, a skilled potter, has been eyeing those goats for weeks, and it just so happens that you've been admiring their beautifully crafted clay pots.

One day, you strike up a conversation and realize that you've got a perfect opportunity for a trade. You offer up two of your finest goats in exchange for a set of pots that would be the pride of any household. Your neighbor jumps at the chance, and just like that, you've both received something you wanted without a single coin changing hands.

Bartering was the go-to way of doing business for thousands of years, from ancient civilizations like the Babylonians and Egyptians to indigenous tribes around the world. It was a simple, effective way to exchange goods and services without the need for a standardized currency.

Of course, there must have been plenty of awkward moments when someone tried to trade a handful of turnips for a new loincloth, or when a particularly stubborn goat refused to be bartered away without a fight. But hey, that's just part of the charm of the barter system – it wasn't always pretty, but it got the job done!

Currency

Now imagine that you're strolling through an ancient Lydian marketplace around 600 B.C. — perusing the wares and trying to score a sweet deal on the latest in toga fashion. Suddenly, you spot the perfect one – it's stylish, it's comfy, and it's just the right shade of purple to make you stand out at the next chariot race. There's just one problem: *you're fresh out of goats.*

In centuries past, this would have been a major bummer, but thanks to those clever Lydians and their newfangled *electrum coins*, you can now simply plunk down a few standardized tokens and walk away with your snazzy new outfit.

This revolutionary concept caught on like wildfire, and soon enough, everyone was trading in their cumbersome bartering goods for shiny, uniform coins. It streamlined commerce, made transactions more efficient, and paved the way for the development of more advanced currency systems.

From there, money continued to evolve. Pure gold and silver coins became the norm, offering even greater standardization and stability. And then, in a move that would have blown the minds of those ancient Lydians, we started using *paper money* – a concept that probably would have seemed about as crazy to them as the idea of carrying around a tiny computer in your pocket that can access the sum of human knowledge.

So the next time you're out shopping and you hand over a crisp bill, take a moment to appreciate those innovative Lydians and their game-changing electrum coins. Without them, you might still be trying to procure sustenance with a slightly confused goat in tow.

Banking

The prototypes of modern banking began in medieval Italy during the 12th and 13th centuries. These early financial institutions were not just places to store gold or silver; they changed the game by introducing fundamental banking services such as lending money at interest. These critical developments fueled economic expansion across Europe, forming the backbone of what would evolve into the intricate, global financial systems we rely on today.

Banking is a big deal. Just imagine daily life without banks—no ATMs for quick cash withdrawals, no online banking services for easy transactions, no safe havens for your hard-earned money. The very thought underscores the profound impact of banking on society. Yet, intriguingly, even in an age dominated by financial technologies, some individuals still opt for traditional methods of saving, like tucking away cash under a mattress, burying repurposed mayo jars in the backyard, or depositing coins into a trusty ceramic swine. To each their own!

Digital Currency

In the 21st century, the concept of money is undergoing yet another radical transformation. The digital era has not only reshaped how we interact with the world but also how we manage and perceive currency. Cryptocurrencies, such as Bitcoin and Ethereum, are reshaping the very foundations of modern banking systems and forcing us to re-evaluate our understanding of money.

The emergence of cryptocurrencies has also introduced a new paradigm in financial transactions, where speed, decentralization, and digital security converge in a powerful trifecta. With a few taps on a smartphone, individuals can now transfer funds across the globe faster than sending an email. It's a compelling era where financial power is quite literally in the hands of the masses, democratizing access to wealth creation and management in ways that were once unimaginable.

Key Financial Terms

Now seems like a good time to lay out some terminology because no matter what form money takes – whether it's a goat, a coin, a bill, or a string of digital code – it's essential to understand how it works.

Income

First up, let's talk about income. This is the money you earn, whether it's from a part-time job, an allowance, or even a side hustle like selling handmade crafts online.

Income can be further broken down 3 different ways:

- **Earned income:** This is money you make from working a job or providing a service. If you babysit on the weekends or work a part-time job, that's earned income.
- **Passive income:** This is money you earn without actively working for it, like earning interest on a savings account or earning royalties from a book you've written.
- **Portfolio income:** This is money you earn from investments, like stocks or bonds. If you own stock in Apple, Coke, or Nike then you'd receive this type of income.

Expenses

Next is the flip side of income: *expenses*. These are all the things you spend money on, from necessities like food and clothing to fun stuff like concert tickets and video games.

There are two main types of expenses to keep in mind:

- **Fixed expenses:** These are costs that generally stay the same each month, like rent, car payments, or a Netflix subscription.
- **Variable expenses:** These are costs that can fluctuate from month to month, like eating out, buying new clothes, or going on a weekend road trip with friends.

Assets vs. Liabilities

Another key concept to understand is the difference between *assets* and *liabilities*. An asset is something you own that has value and can potentially produce an income, like money in a savings account, a piece of real estate, or even a rare collectible item. A liability, on the other hand, is something that costs you money, like a credit card balance, a car payment, or a student loan.

To build long-term wealth, it's important to focus on acquiring assets and minimizing liabilities. Think of it this way: every dollar you save and invest is like a little seed that can grow into a big, beautiful money tree over time. But every dollar you spend on liabilities is one less seed you have that has the potential to grow—it's gone forever.

Perceived Value Of Currency

Money, in essence, has value because we all buy into the belief that it does. This is what's known as *"perceived value"*—the notion that something is worth whatever everyone thinks it's worth, rather than any real, tangible value.

Consider the humble $100 bill. In simplest terms, it's a paper rectangle with a picture of a dead guy on it. Is it *actually worth* $100? Not even close. Unlike a gold coin or a diamond, a dollar bill doesn't have any tangible value beyond perhaps that of a makeshift bookmark. But because we all agree to treat this fancy paper as something precious, we can wield its mighty "perceived" power to buy groceries.

This concept is crucial because it reveals that money's value can swing like a pendulum based on the whims of economic and social trends. So next time you hold a bill, remember, it's not just paper—it's a collective pinky promise within our society!

Economic Principals

Now that we've covered some of the key concepts related to money and financial literacy, let's zoom out a bit and talk about how larger economic principles can impact your personal finances. Don't worry – we're not going to get too bogged down in academic jargon or complex graphs. Instead, we'll focus on only two concepts that are essential to understand as you navigate your financial journey.

Supply & Demand

This fundamental concept dictates that the price of a good or service is determined by its availability (supply) and how much everyone is clamoring to get it (demand).

Picture this: when there's a mountain of something and no one's particularly desperate for it, the price is as low as a limbo stick at Bilbo Baggin's beach party.

On the flip side, when something is scarce, and everyone wants a piece, prices climb faster than an orangutan on Red Bull.

Inflation

One of the sneakiest villains in the world of money is inflation, a silent beast that creeps into your wallet and plays havoc with the purchasing power of your hard-earned cash.

Here's how it works:

As the price of goods and services rises, the value of money falls.

Suppose you've got $10 tucked away in your wallet. Today, that crisp tenner could net you a couple of those overpriced lattes or maybe a shiny new paperback to add to your collection. But give inflation a few years to do its thing, and watch what happens. That same $10 might barely purchase a single latte or, at best, snag a dog-eared novel from the bargain bin.

This creeping currency conundrum is why it's crucial to put your money to work by purchasing assets or investing! Think of it as training your dollars to fight off inflation and protect their purchasing power.

Investing wisely, whether in stocks, bonds, or mutant squirrel farms *(just seeing if you're paying attention)*, helps ensure that your money grows muscles, keeping pace with or even outrunning inflation. That way, your future self can enjoy more than just half a coffee and a faded cover!

ACTIVITY: "Basics-Of-Money" Quiz

1. What is the difference between earned income and passive income? a. Earned income is money you make from working, while passive income is money you earn without actively working for it. b. Earned income is money you earn from investments, while passive income is money you make from a job. c. There is no difference between earned income and passive income.

2. Which of the following is an example of a fixed expense? a. Buying a new pair of shoes b. Going out to dinner with friends c. Paying your monthly car insurance bill

3. What does it mean when we say that money has "perceived value"? a. Money is backed by a tangible asset, like gold or silver. b. Money is worth what people collectively agree it's worth, rather than having any inherent value. c. Money has no real value and is just a social construct.

4. How can inflation impact your purchasing power over time? a. Inflation makes your money more valuable over time, so you can buy more with it. b. Inflation has no impact on your purchasing power. c. Inflation can decrease your purchasing power over time, as prices rise while the value of your money stays the same.

5. What is an example of an Asset? a. A brand new smartphone b. Your Netflix subscription c. A silver coin.

Answer Key: 1a, 2c, 3b, 4c, 5c

Chapter 2

Earning Your Own Money

The only place success comes before work is in the dictionary. —Vince Lombardi

When you earn your own money, you're taking a big step towards financial independence and responsibility. You're also learning valuable skills that will serve you well throughout your life, like time management, communication, and problem-solving.

So, what are some ways to earn money as a teenager? We'll talk about many different options, ranging from simpler jobs for younger teens to more advanced opportunities for older, more experienced teens. There's a smorgasbord of opportunities for everyone, so let's get right into it.

Household Responsibilities & Earning Opportunities

Ah, the illustrious teenage years! A time of growth, rebellion, and... learning how to load a dishwasher properly. Yes, dear young compatriot, as you navigate the treacherous waters of teendom, you'll find yourself embarking on the noble quest of household chores. Fear not, for these tasks are not mere drudgery, but stepping stones on your path to adulthood *(and perhaps a well-organized sock drawer)*.

Picture, if you will, the humble abode you call home - a veritable kingdom of dust bunnies and misplaced remote controls. As a junior member of this domestic realm, your charge is to aid in its upkeep. Why, you ask? Well, beyond the obvious goal of preventing your living space from being mistaken for a post-apocalyptic wasteland, these responsibilities serve a greater purpose.

By mastering the art of vacuuming and tackling the enigma that is folding fitted sheets, you're doing more than just sprucing up your living space—you're actually building a toolkit of life skills that'll come in handy long after the dust settles. Think of it as a crash course in teamwork, time management, and the subtle science of laundry preservation. Who knew that learning to rescue your favorite t-shirt from a dryer-induced miniaturization could be so valuable?

Now, here's where things get tricky: what constitutes a standard family duty versus an opportunity to line your pockets?

In the Johnson household, young Timmy might be expected to feed the family's pet iguana as part of his regular duties. Meanwhile, across the street, the Smiths might consider iguana-feeding an exotic task worthy of monetary compensation. The key is to engage in that most ancient and revered of family traditions: the household negotiation. Approach your parental units with the grace of a diplomat in order to gain clarity on what tasks represent income earning opportunities.

Regular chores might include:

- Keeping your bedroom clean
- Participating in the daily ritual of washing dishes
- Feeding and watering the family pet(s)
- Maintaining shared living spaces

Tasks that might fatten your piggy bank:

- Taming the jungle that is your backyard
- Washing & detailing the family car
- Cleaning and organizing the garage
- Pressure-washing the driveway

Now, before you start seeing dollar signs every time you pick up a broom, let's talk about the elephant in the room *(which, by the way, you should probably dust)*. Not every household task should come with a price tag. If they did, you'd be missing out on some pretty crucial life lessons.

Contributing to your household without expecting payment is part of being in a family. It's about pulling your weight, showing appreciation for the roof over your head, and learning to be a responsible human being. If you got paid for every dish you washed or every sock you paired, you'd be learning the wrong lesson—that you should only help out when there's something in it for you.

It's all about finding the right balance. Maybe routine chores are your family contribution, but bigger projects or extra efforts could be opportunities to earn some dough. The key is to approach it with the right attitude—one of willingness to help and contribute, not just for your own, personal benefit.

Remember, the skills and values you're developing—responsibility, work ethic, time management—are worth **far more** than a few bucks here and there. They're the foundation for your future success, whether you're aiming to be the CEO of a Fortune 500 company or the world's greatest dog walker.

So, as you navigate the world of chores and responsibilities, keep this in mind: sometimes, the most valuable rewards aren't the ones that jingle in your pocket. They're the ones that shape you into a capable, responsible, and considerate adult. That's a payoff that'll keep on giving long after you've mastered the art of loading a dishwasher.

Part-Time Jobs

One of the most traditional ways for teens to earn money is through part-time jobs. Whether it's slinging hash at a local diner, selling the latest fashion at a retail store, or surviving the chaos of summer camp—part-time jobs offer a fantastic way to gain work experience and earn a steady paycheck without totally ruining your social life.

But how do you find these mythical part-time jobs? Start by considering your interests and skills. Fancy yourself a future tech mogul? Look for opportunities at electronics stores or IT support centers. Have a knack for keeping two-year-olds entertained? Consider applying for a job at a daycare center. What do you enjoy? What are you good at?

Don't forget to scour online job boards like Indeed or Snagajob, which often feature sections dedicated to teen jobs. And tap into your personal network—inform your friends, family, and teachers that you're on the hunt. They might know someone, who knows someone, who knows someone else who's looking for the next great part-time, teenage employee.

Finally, walk right into local businesses and see if they're hiring. Many small businesses love to hire teens, especially those who demonstrate the initiative to actively seek out work.

Filling Out An Application

When you find a job that interests you, it's time to start the application process. Even if you don't have much work experience, you can still create a strong resume and cover letter.

Focus on highlighting your strengths, like your academic achievements, extracurricular activities, or volunteer work. If you've helped out with any school projects or community events, be sure to mention those, too!

Here are a few tips to make your application stand out:

1. Tailor your resume and cover letter to the specific job you're applying for. Show how your skills and experiences match what the employer is looking for.
2. Use action verbs to describe your achievements, like "led," "organized," or "created."
3. Double-check your spelling and grammar, and ask a trusted adult to review your application before you submit it.

4. If possible, include a reference or two, like a teacher or coach who can speak to your work ethic and character.

Once you land an interview, it's essential to prepare. Research the company and think about how your skills and experiences align with the job requirements. Practice common interview questions with a friend or family member, and don't forget to dress professionally and arrive on time.

During the interview, be sure to:

- Make eye contact and offer a firm handshake.
- Listen carefully to the questions and take a moment to think before answering.
- Provide specific examples of times when you've demonstrated the skills or qualities they're looking for.
- Ask questions of your own to show your interest and enthusiasm for the job.

Remember, every interview is a learning opportunity, even if you don't get the job. Ask for feedback on how you can improve, and stay positive – the right opportunity will inevitably come your way.

The Gig Economy and Freelancing

If traditional part-time jobs aren't your thing, don't worry – there are plenty of other ways to earn money as a teenager. One option that's become increasingly popular in recent years is the gig economy and freelancing.

So, what exactly is the gig economy? Essentially, it refers to a labor market characterized by short-term contracts or freelance work, as opposed to permanent, full-time jobs. Thanks to the internet and digital platforms, it's easier than ever for people to find and offer freelance services.

By the way, in 2023, the global value of the gig economy was estimated to be $455.2 billion dollars and is only expected to continue growing in value. What that means is that there's *a lot of money* to be made by those who have the necessary skills and know-how, so let's explore this in more detail.

Freelance Platforms

Some popular gig and freelance platforms for teens include Fiverr, Upwork, and TaskRabbit. On these sites, you can create a profile showcasing your skills and services, whether it's graphic design, writing, or even doing odd jobs like assembling furniture or running errands.

Let's say you're a whiz at social media and have a knack for creating engaging posts. You could offer your services on Fiverr as a social media manager for small businesses or entrepreneurs. Or maybe you're a talented artist who could design custom logos or illustrations on Upwork. The opportunities are virtually endless.

Building A Portfolio

To be successful in the gig economy, it's important to build a strong portfolio that showcases your work and attracts potential clients. Start by taking on a few small projects and asking for testimonials and reviews from satisfied customers. As you gain more experience and positive feedback, you can start to raise your rates and take on more significant projects.

Here are a few tips for creating a standout freelance profile:

1. Choose a clear, professional profile picture and username.
2. Write a compelling bio that highlights your skills, experience, and unique selling points.
3. Include samples or links to your best work, and make sure they're up-to-date and relevant to the services you're offering.
4. Set competitive rates based on your experience and the market demand for your services.
5. Be responsive to client inquiries and maintain clear communication throughout each project.

Of course, managing gig work can be a bit different than a traditional part-time job. You'll need to be proactive about finding and applying for gigs, and you'll also need to manage your own time and workload. It's important to set realistic deadlines, communicate clearly with clients, and deliver high-quality work to build a positive reputation.

Learning Valuable "Gig" Skills

With online learning platforms like Udemy, you can take a variety of courses that can teach you valuable gig skills. There are near-countless courses to peruse and take, but here are some general ideas of valuable skills you may want to look into that will come in handy if you'd like to start taking on some gigs.

Word Processing: Young scholars can learn the ins and outs of Microsoft Word and Google Docs. These aren't just nifty skills for acing that English paper—they're also in hot demand in the freelance market.

Picture this: You, the master of fonts, the ruler of margins, the sultan of spacing. Your skills are in high demand, and local publishing houses are practically begging for your expertise. They need someone who can wrangle those pesky formatting issues and make their documents look like a million bucks. And guess what? That someone could be you!

Graphic Design: Ever judged a book by its cover? Well, buckle up, buttercup, because now you can be the one behind those covers, pulling the strings and making the magic happen!

Enter the dazzling world of graphic design, where you'll transform from a mere mortal into a visual virtuoso. With the power of Adobe Photoshop at your fingertips, you'll be turning bland into brand faster than you can say "CMYK."

Whether you're crafting the next iconic logo that'll be plastered on everything from billboards to t-shirts, or simply trying to make your mom's bake sale flyer look less like a ransom note, these skills will have you stacking the aesthetic deck in your favor.

With great design power comes great responsibility. Use your newfound abilities wisely, and soon you'll be the one everyone turns to when they need a visual makeover.

Digital Marketing: In the vast and ever-expanding digital kingdom, marketing reigns supreme as the queen, with content as her trusty king. And guess what? You, my young friend, can become a key player in this royal court!

Digital marketing is all about mastering the art of advertising for businesses on the wild, wild web—and driving sales with your trusty tools of SEO talent and social media savvy.

And let's be real, you teens are practically born with smartphones in your hands. You've been tweeting, sharing, and liking since you could crawl. Why not put those skills to work and turn them into a lucrative gig or even launch your own digital marketing empire?

Coding and Web Development: Listen up, digital dynamos! It's time to unveil the true power behind our online realm: *code*.

With coding skills, you're not just another face in the digital crowd—you're the mastermind, the architect, the wizard wielding a secret language that makes computers bow to your will.

These days, coding isn't just a skill; it's a superpower. Imagine creating websites so slick they make users weep with joy or apps so addictive people forget their basic human needs. And the best part? It pays, and pays very well.

So, what are you waiting for? Dive into coding and unlock the secrets of our digital domain. Who knows? You might just create the next big thing that takes the internet by storm.

Video Editing and Production: Lights, camera, action! In the wild world of social media, video content is the undisputed king of the jungle. And you, my friend, can be the one sitting pretty in the director's chair with the power of video editing at your fingertips.

With video editing skills, you're not just another content creator; you're a visual alchemist, mixing and matching clips, adding special effects, and weaving together narratives that make people laugh, cry, or gasp in awe. You have the power to create videos that go viral faster than a cat playing the piano, a cat eating snow, or a cat scared of it's reflection... really almost any cat video.

In today's attention economy, video is the currency that rules them all. From YouTube to TikTok, Instagram to Facebook, video content is what keeps the masses glued to their screens. Why settle for being a mere spectator, watching viral videos from the sidelines, when you can be the one behind the camera, pulling the strings and making the magic happen?

Entrepreneurship for Teens

For some teens, the ultimate dream is to be their own boss and start a business. While it might sound intimidating (*gulp), entrepreneurship can be an exciting and rewarding way to earn money and gain valuable experience.

The first step in starting a business is to generate and validate your idea. What products or services are you passionate about? Is there a need or demand for them in your community? Do some market research to see what similar businesses are out there and how you can differentiate yourself.

Let's say you're an avid baker and have always dreamed of starting your own cookie delivery service. You could start by surveying your friends, family, and neighbors to gauge interest and get feedback on your product. You might even offer free samples to get people hooked on your delicious treats!

Once you have a solid idea, it's time to start business planning. This means outlining your product or service, identifying your target market, developing marketing strategies, and creating financial projections.

Don't worry if this sounds overwhelming – there are plenty of resources and templates available online to help guide you through the process.

One helpful tool is the Business Model Canvas, which is a simple template that helps you visualize and plan the key components of your business. It includes sections for your value proposition, customer segments, revenue streams, and more. You can find free templates online or even create your own using a spreadsheet or slide presentation.

As you develop your business plan, be sure to think about your start-up costs and how you'll fund your venture. Will you need to purchase equipment or supplies? Will you need to rent a space or hire employees? How much will you charge for your products or services, and how many units do you need to sell to break even?

It's also important to think about your marketing and sales strategies. How will you get the word out about your business? Will you use social media, flyers, or word-of-mouth referrals? How will you process orders and payments, and deliver your products or services to customers?

Now, I know this sounds like a lot to figure out — *and it is*, but starting your own business can be incredibly rewarding. Not only will you have the opportunity to earn money doing something you love, but you'll also gain valuable skills in leadership, problem-solving, and communication. Plus, you'll have a unique story and experience to share with future employers or college admissions officers.

A Teen Entrepreneur

Take the example of Jordan, a 17-year-old who started his own lawn care business last spring. He began by mowing lawns for his neighbors on weekends, but quickly expanded his services to include landscaping and yard clean-up. With the help of his parents, he invested in some basic equipment and created a simple website and social media pages to promote his business.

Within a few months, Jordan had a steady stream of clients and was earning enough money to save for college and even hire a few friends to help with bigger projects. He learned how to manage his time, communicate with customers, and handle the financial aspects of running a business. Now, he's considering studying entrepreneurship in college and dreams of owning his own full-fledged commercial landscaping company one day.

The sky's the limit when it comes to entrepreneurship, so don't be afraid to dream big and take risks. With hard work, creativity, and a willingness to learn, you can turn your passions into a profitable business.

ACTIVITY: Create A Business Plan

Now that we've explored some different ways to earn money as a teenager, it's time for you to put these ideas into action! Here's a fun activity to get you started:

Choose a small business idea that aligns with your skills and interests. This could be tutoring, pet-sitting, lawn care, washing cars, or anything else you're passionate about.

Create a simple business plan that includes:

1. A description of your service (mowing lawns, baking cookies, etc.)
2. Your target market (who will your customers be?)
3. Your pricing strategy (monthly service, pay per product, etc.)
4. A basic marketing plan (Door flyers, newspaper ad, etc))
5. A goal for your earnings (how much do you hope to make?)

By creating this basic plan, you'll gain practical experience in thinking like an entrepreneur and setting financial goals. Who knows – this activity could be the first step towards starting your own successful business!

Chapter 3
The Art Of Budgeting

A budget is people telling their money where to go instead of wondering where it went. —John Maxwell

Imagine this: Your friend Alex has been saving up for months to buy a new phone and she's finally got enough to make the purchase, but on her way to the store, her car breaks down. It's an unfortunate event, but one that she's ready to handle because Alex has a budget.

As part of her budget, she set aside $20 a month from her part-time babysitting job as an *"emergency fund"*. It's because she planned ahead and maintained a budget that she was able to dip into her emergency savings, fix her car, and carry on with her plan to purchase a new phone.

This would have been a different situation if she had not budgeted her money well. Without her emergency fund, she would have needed to pay for repairs rather than get her new phone, which would have been a real bummer. Not Alex though — she was prepared and armed with a budget that helped her easily navigate life's inevitable twists and turns.

Why Budgeting Matters

If your money were a car, budgeting would be the GPS that helps you navigate to your destination. Without a GPS, you're just driving aimlessly, hoping you'll end up somewhere good.

But with a well-planned budget, you have a clear sense of direction to your financial goals, whether that's saving up for a new laptop, starting a college fund, or even planning for your future dream home.

Budgeting gives you the power to decide where your money goes, rather than wondering where it went.

Budgeting isn't just about reaching your goals. It's also about reducing financial stress and anxiety. When you have a clear picture of your income and expenses, you're less likely to be caught off guard by unexpected bills or run into debt trouble. You can plan ahead, save for emergencies, and even treat yourself occasionally, all without worrying that you're jeopardizing your financial future.

Think about it this way: when you're in school, you probably have a planner or calendar to keep track of your assignments, exams, and extracurricular activities. You wouldn't just wing it and hope for the best, right? The same goes for your money. By creating a budget and sticking to it, you're setting yourself up for success both now and in the future.

Understanding Income

The first step in creating a budget is to get a clear picture of your income. This might include:

- Allowance from your parents or guardians
- Money from a part-time job or online gig
- Birthday or holiday cash gifts
- Cash earned from washing cars

Take a moment to list out all your income streams and add them up to determine your total monthly income. If your income varies from month to month (like if you work odd hours at your part-time job), try to estimate an average monthly amount.

It's important to be honest and realistic about your income. Don't inflate the numbers or count on money that you don't actually have coming in. The goal is to create a budget based on your real financial situation, not an idealized version of it.

Tracking Your Expenses

Now that you know how much money you have coming in each month, it's time to take a look at where that money is going. This is where tracking your expenses comes in.

Start by listing out all your regular monthly expenses, like:

- School lunches or supplies
- Clothing or personal care items
- Transportation costs (like gas money or bus fare)
- Phone or internet bills

- Subscription services (like Netflix)
- Entertainment expenses (like movie tickets or video games)

Don't forget to include any irregular expenses that come up throughout the year, like birthday gifts for friends or family, vacations, or school trips.

Categorizing Expenses

Once you have a complete list of your expenses, try categorizing them into "*needs*" (essential expenses, like school supplies), "*wants*" (non-essential expenses, like eating out or buying new clothes), and "s*avings*" (money you set aside for future goals or emergencies).

This categorization process can help you identify areas where you might be overspending and opportunities to cut back. For example, if you notice that you're spending a lot of money on fast food or coffee shops, you could try packing your own lunches or brewing your own coffee at home to save money.

Remember, tracking your expenses isn't about judging yourself or feeling guilty about your spending. It's simply a way to bring awareness to your financial habits and make informed decisions about where you want your money to go.

Setting Financial Goals

One of the key benefits of budgeting is that it allows you to set and achieve financial goals. These could be short-term goals, like saving up for a new phone or a summer road trip, or long-term goals, like saving for college or a car.

Take some time to think about your financial goals and write them down. Be specific and realistic – instead of just saying "*save money,*" set a concrete goal like "*save $500 for a new laptop by the end of the year.*"

Once you have your goals in mind, incorporate them into your budget. Determine how much money you need to save each month to reach your goal, and treat that savings amount as a non-negotiable "expense" in your budget.

Having clear financial goals can help you stay motivated and focused when it comes to budgeting. Instead of feeling like you're depriving yourself, you'll know that every dollar you save is bringing you one step closer to achieving your goals.

Choosing a Budgeting Method

Now that you have a clear picture of your income, expenses, and financial goals, it's time to choose a budgeting method that works for you. Here are a few popular options:

1. **The 50/30/20 rule:** This method suggests allocating 50% of your income to needs *(like rent, utilities, and that pesky expense called "food")*, 30% to wants *(like those new shoes you've been eyeing or that fancy dinner out with friends)*, and 20% to savings and debt repayment *(because your future self will thank you)*. It's a simple and effective way to ensure you're covering your essentials while still leaving room for fun and future planning.
2. **The envelope system:** With this method, you physically divide your cash into different envelopes labeled with each expense category (like "groceries,"

"entertainment," or "savings"). Each category is allowed a specific dollar amount of your choosing. This system can be especially helpful if you tend to overspend in certain areas. Just be sure to keep your cash-filled envelopes in a safe place. You wouldn't want your "grocery fund" mysteriously disappearing before your next trip to the supermarket.

3. **Budgeting apps and spreadsheets:** There are tons of digital tools available to help you track your income and expenses, set goals, and monitor your progress. Some popular options include Mint, YNAB (You Need a Budget), and PocketGuard. You can also create your own simple budget spreadsheet using Google Sheets or Microsoft Excel.

Ultimately, the best budgeting method is the one that you'll actually stick with. It may take some trial and error to find a system that works for you, and that's okay! The most important thing is to choose a method that aligns with your personality, lifestyle, and financial goals.

Sticking to Your Budget

Creating a budget is one thing – sticking to it is another. It takes discipline, commitment, and a willingness to make tough choices sometimes. But trust me, the rewards of living within your means and achieving your financial goals are so worth it!

Here are a few tips for sticking to your budget:

1. **Track your spending:** Keep a close eye on where your money is going. You can use a budgeting app, a spreadsheet, or even a simple notebook to log your purchases.
2. **Review and adjust your budget regularly:** Set aside time each month to review your budget and see how you're doing. If you notice that you're consistently overspending in one category or have extra money left over in another, make adjustments as needed.
3. **Celebrate successes & learn from your setbacks:** Budgeting is a skill that takes practice – don't beat yourself up if you make mistakes along the way. Instead, celebrate your wins (like hitting a savings goal or staying within your budget for a whole month) and use your setbacks as opportunities to learn and improve.

Remember, sticking to a budget isn't about depriving yourself of all joy and fun. It's about being intentional with your money and using it in a way that aligns with your values and goals.

Dealing with Unexpected Expenses

No matter how well you plan, life has a way of surprising us at the most unexpected of times. Whether it's a car repair, a medical bill, or a last-minute school expense, unexpected costs can put a serious strain on your budget.

That's why it's so important to have an emergency fund — a separate savings account that you can tap into when the unexpected happens. Aim to save up at least $500 to $1,000 in your emergency fund, or enough to cover one to two months' worth of expenses. Think of it as a financial safety net, ready to catch you when life decides to give you a shove off the trapeze.

If an unexpected expense comes up and you don't have enough saved in your emergency fund, don't panic. See if you can adjust your budget temporarily to accommodate the extra cost. Just remember, a little sacrifice now can save you from a world of financial pain later.

If the expense is too big to handle on your own, talk to your parents or a trusted adult about your options. They might have some wisdom to share or be able to offer some short-term assistance to get you back on your financial feet.

The key is to anticipate the unexpected as much as possible and have a plan in place to handle it. That way, when life throws you a financial curveball, you'll be ready to swing for the fences. With a little forethought and preparation, you'll be able to handle whatever comes your way.

Budgeting Tips for Teens

Budgeting as a teenager comes with its own unique set of challenges and opportunities. Here are a few tips to help you make the most of your budgeting journey:

Involve your parents or guardians

If you're still living at home, it's helpful to involve your parents or guardians in your budgeting process. They can offer valuable guidance, help you track your expenses, and even provide incentives for achieving your financial goals. Plus, being open about your finances now can set the stage for healthy money conversations in the future.

Find ways to increase your income

If you're struggling to make your budget work, consider looking for ways to boost your income. This could mean taking on additional shifts at your part-time job, starting a side hustle (like tutoring or pet-sitting), taking on some online gig projects, or selling items you no longer need.

Identifying "Needs" vs. "Wants"

It's all too easy to get caught up in the latest trends or feel pressure to keep up with your friend's spending habits. But learning to distinguish between "*needs*" (things you can't live without) and "*wants*" (things that are nice to have but not essential) is a key part of successful budgeting. Before making a purchase, ask yourself – is this something I truly need, or just something I want in the moment?

Avoiding Common Budgeting Mistakes:

To wrap up this chapter, here are a few common pitfalls that can derail even the best-laid budgeting plans.

These include:

- Not tracking your expenses regularly
- Not setting clear financial goals
- Not adjusting your budget as your circumstances change
- Not having an emergency fund for unexpected expenses

- Comparing yourself to others or trying to keep up with unsustainable spending habits

By being aware of these potential mistakes and taking steps to avoid them, you'll be well on your way to budgeting success.

ACTIVITY: Create Your Budget

Now that you've learned the basics of budgeting, it's time to put your knowledge into practice! Follow these steps to create your own personal budget:

Step 1: Income

- List all your sources of income (allowance, part-time job, birthday gifts, etc.)
- Calculate your total monthly income.

Step 2: Expenses

- List all your monthly expenses (needs, wants, and savings).
- Categorize each expense as a need, want, or savings.
- Add up your total expenses for each category.

Step 3: Compare

- Subtract your total expenses from your total income.
- If you have money left over *(cha-ching!)*, allocate it to your savings or financial goals.
- If your expenses exceed your income *(fear not!),* look for areas to cut back or ways to increase your income.

Step 4: Choose a Budgeting Method

- Decide on a budgeting method that works for you (50/30/20 rule, envelope system, or digital tools).
- Allocate your income to each expense category based on your chosen method.

Step 5: Set Goals

- Write down your short-term and long-term financial goals.
- Determine how much you need to save each month to reach your goals.
- Incorporate your goal savings into your budget.

Step 6: Review and Adjust

- Track your income and expenses throughout the month.
- At the end of the month, review your budget to see how you did.
- Make adjustments as needed based on your progress and any changes in your financial situation.

Remember, your budget is a dynamic system that *absolutely should* adapt to your changing circumstances, so don't be afraid to make adjustments as needed. The goal is to find a balance that works for you and helps you achieve your financial objectives.

Chapter 4
Saving For The Future

Compound interest is the eighth wonder of the world. He who understands it earns it; he who doesn't pays it.
— Albert Einstein

Every dollar you save today is a gift to your future self. It's a promise that you'll have the resources you need to chase your dreams, weather unexpected challenges, and live life on your own terms. But here's the most important thing I can tell you about saving — *the earlier you start, the better.*

Take the story of Wyatt; he's 26 now, but when he was 14 years old, he started saving $50 a month from a part-time job. At first, it wasn't easy – he had to cut back on spending, and that meant saying *"no"* when it would have felt so much better to say *"yes"*. Fast forward 10 years, and Wyatt's savings have grown to over $9,000, thanks to the power of *compound interest*. His savings allowed him to pay cash for his first car and eventually put a downpayment on his first house — all because he made the choice to *start saving early.*

The Power of Compound Interest

Compound interest is the interest you earn on **both** your initial savings **and** the interest those savings have already earned.

Let's break it down with a few examples that build on each other using an easy-to-calculate interest rate of 5%:

$100 at 5% for 1 year

Say you put $100 into a savings account that earns 5% interest per year. After the first year, you'll have $105 – your original $100, plus $5 in interest. Nothing to get too excited about, but that's just the beginning...

$100 at 5% for 10 years

Now, imagine that you leave $100 in your savings account for 10 years. Compound interest will turn that $100 into about $163. That's over 63% growth, without you having to lift a finger! Now we're getting somewhere, but it gets much better...

$100 at 5% for 10 years with contributions

Instead of simply leaving $100 in your savings account all by its lonesome, *imagine that you faithfully contribute $50 each month.*

In ten years, your initial $100 investment would quietly swell to about $7,836. Of that amount, $1,736 is from interest alone! This tidy sum reflects not just your consistent monthly contributions but also the sneaky power of compound interest working its magic in the background, proving that regular savings, even in small doses, can grow impressively over time.

Types of Savings Accounts

Now that you understand the power of compound interest, let's talk about where you can put your savings to maximize its growth potential. There are several different types of savings accounts, each with its own pros and cons.

Vanilla Savings Account

This is probably the account you think of when you hear the word "savings". It's a simple account where you can deposit money and earn a small amount of interest. These accounts are easy to open and give you quick access to your cash when you need it. However, their interest rates tend to be pretty low, often much less than 1%.

High-Yield Savings Account

If you're looking for a bit more bang for your buck, you might consider a high-yield savings account. These accounts typically offer much higher interest rates than traditional savings accounts – sometimes 10 or 20 times higher! The catch is that they often require a larger minimum balance and may have restrictions on how often you can withdraw funds.

Say you have $1,000 to put into savings. If you put that money in a traditional savings account earning 1% interest, you'd earn $10 over the course of a year. But if you put that same $1,000 in a high-yield savings account earning 5% interest, you'd earn $50 in a year – *that's 5x the yield just by choosing a different savings account!*

Certificate of Deposit

Another option is a certificate of deposit, or CD. With a CD, you agree to leave your money in the account for a set period of time, usually anywhere from a few months to a few years. In exchange, you'll typically earn a higher interest rate than you would with a regular savings account. The interest rate is often around 3%. The downside is that if you need to access your money before the CD term is up, you'll likely face a penalty.

CDs can be a great option if you have a chunk of money that you know you won't need for a while. By locking in a higher interest rate for a set term, you can maximize your savings growth without the temptation to spend the money prematurely.

One strategy to maximize the benefits of CDs while maintaining some flexibility is called "CD laddering." This involves spreading your money across multiple CDs with different maturity dates. For example, instead of putting $5,000 in a single 5-year CD, you might put $1,000 each in 1-year, 2-year, 3-year, 4-year, and 5-year CDs. As each CD matures, you can either withdraw the money if needed or reinvest it in a new 5-year CD, potentially at a higher interest rate. This approach allows you to take advantage of higher long-term rates while still having regular access to a portion of your funds.

How to Choose?

So, which type of account is right for you? It really depends on your individual savings goals and circumstances. If you need easy access to your money and aren't too worried about maximizing interest, a basic savings account might be the way to go. If you have a larger sum to save, want to earn more interest, and know you won't need access to the money for a while, then a high-yield account or CD could be the smart choice.

The key is to do your research and shop around. Compare interest rates, fees, and minimum balance requirements from different banks and credit unions. And remember, you don't have to put all your eggs in one basket. You can use a combination of different accounts to meet your various savings needs and goals.

For example, you might keep your emergency fund in a high-yield savings account for easy access and higher returns, while putting your car savings in a CD to lock in a good rate. The point is to be strategic and intentional with where you stash your cash.

Setting Savings Goals

Let's talk about how to set effective savings targets. After all, saving money is a lot easier when you have a clear idea of what you're saving for and why.

One popular framework for goal-setting is the SMART criteria. This stands for **S**pecific, **M**easurable, **A**chievable, **R**elevant, and **T**ime-bound.

Let's break down each of these components:

- **Specific:** Your savings goal should be clearly defined and focused. Instead of saying, *"I want to save money,"* try something like, *"I want to save $500 for a summer road trip."*

- **Measurable:** Your goal should be quantifiable so you can track your progress. "*Save $500*" is much more measurable than "*save some money.*"
- **Achievable:** Make sure your goal is realistic and attainable, given your current financial situation. If you're working part-time and have a lot of expenses, saving $10,000 in a year might not be feasible.
- **Relevant:** Your savings goal should be meaningful and aligned with your values and priorities. If travel isn't important to you, saving for a big road trip might not be the most motivating goal.
- **Time-bound:** Finally, your goal should have a clear deadline. This helps create a sense of urgency and accountability. "*Save $500 by June*" is much more powerful than "*save $500.*"

If your savings goal fits within the SMART framework, you're far more likely to achieve the goal. Let's put this into action with a real-life example.

Meet Liam, a 15-year-old who loves photography. Liam's dream is to buy a high-quality camera to take his hobby to the next level. Using the SMART framework, Liam sets his savings goal:

"I will save $750 to buy the Canon EOS Rebel T7 camera bundle within 8 months, by December 31st. I will do this by saving $94 per month from my part-time tutoring job and birthday money."

See how specific and actionable Liam's goal is? He's not just saving for a vague "camera" – he's identified the exact make and model he wants, along with a clear price target and timeline. By breaking his goal down into monthly increments, he's created a roadmap for success that is perfectly achievable.

Staying On Track

Of course, setting a goal is just the first step. To stay on track, you'll need to regularly monitor your progress and make adjustments as needed. One helpful strategy is to visualize your savings growth using charts or graphs. Many banking and budgeting apps have built-in tools for this, or you can create your own using a spreadsheet.

Saving For Multiple Things

Another key to successful saving is balancing multiple goals. Let's face it, you probably have more than one thing you want to save for – maybe you're eyeing a new phone, planning for college, and dreaming of a post-graduation trip all at the same time. The key is to prioritize your goals based on importance and timeline and to allocate your savings accordingly.

One approach is to divide your savings into different categories for each goal. For example, you might have a "car fund," a "college fund," and a "fun fund." Each month, you'll allocate a portion of your savings to each category based on your priorities and timeline.

This not only helps you stay organized and motivated, but it also ensures that you're making progress on all your goals, not just the most pressing or exciting ones. And remember, it's okay to adjust your goals and priorities as your life changes. The key is to stay flexible and keep saving, no matter what.

Emergency Funds

In addition to saving for specific goals, there's one type of savings that everyone should have: *an emergency fund.* This is a stash of cash set aside specifically for unexpected expenses or financial setbacks, like a car repair, medical bill, or job loss.

Having an emergency fund is like wearing a seatbelt – you hope you never need it, but if you do, it could save you from serious harm. Without an emergency cushion, you might be forced to rely on credit cards or loans to cover sudden costs, which can quickly spiral into debt. Or, you might have to raid your other savings goals, setting you back on your financial journey.

Let's look at a real-world scenario. Consider Sophia, a 19-year-old college student who got into a fender bender and needed to pay a $500 insurance deductible to get her car fixed. If Sophia didn't have an emergency fund, she would have needed to put that $500 on a high-interest credit card. That $500 credit charge could eventually amount to hundreds more in interest if she were only able to make the minimum payment. Thankfully, Sophia planned ahead and set up an emergency fund, which allowed her to tap into savings to cover the deductible without going into debt or sacrificing her other financial goals.

How much to save?

So, how much should you have in your emergency fund? A good rule of thumb is to save enough to cover 3 to 6 months' worth of essential living expenses. This includes things like rent/mortgage, food, utilities, transportation, and insurance – basically, the bare minimum you need to get by.

To calculate your emergency fund target, add up your essential monthly costs and multiply by either 3 or 6, depending on how much of a cushion you prefer to have. For example, if your core expenses are $1,000 a month, you'll want to aim for an emergency fund of $3,000-$6,000.

I know that might seem like a daunting number, especially if you're just starting your savings journey. But remember, you don't have to build your emergency fund overnight. Start small, with whatever you can afford to set aside each month, and make it a priority to contribute regularly to your emergency fund over time.

How to fund it?

One strategy is to treat your emergency fund like an expense, just like rent or utilities. Include it in your budget and automate your contributions so you're saving without even thinking about it. And when you get a windfall, like a tax refund or birthday cash, consider putting a portion directly into your emergency stash.

Where to keep it?

As for where to keep your emergency fund, you'll want to choose an account that's safe, accessible, and earns at least a little bit of interest. A high-yield savings account is usually a good bet, just avoid accounts with high fees or minimum balance requirements, and make sure you can access your money quickly if needed.

The key is to build your emergency fund consistently over time and resist the temptation to dip into it for non-emergencies. You don't want to be like the trapeze artist who, on a whim, decided to trade in their safety net for a fancy new sequin leotard. Sure, they looked fabulous soaring through the air in dazzling fashion, but if a slip occurred...

Savings and Technology

In today's digital age, technology has made saving easier and more convenient than ever before. From budgeting apps to online savings accounts, there are countless tools at your fingertips to help you reach your financial goals.

Automatic Savings

As mentioned in the last chapter, apps like Mint and YNAB (You Need A Budget) help you create and stick to a budget by tracking your income, expenses, and savings goals. They offer features like bill reminders, spending alerts, and personalized recommendations to keep you on track.

Another handy tool is spare change investing apps, such as Acorns or Stash. These apps round up your purchases to the nearest dollar and invest the spare change into a diversified portfolio. Over time, these small investments can add up to significant savings without you even noticing the money leaving your account.

Tracking Progress

Another benefit of technology is the ability to track your progress in real-time. With just a few taps on your phone, you can see exactly how much you've saved, how much you have left to reach your goal, and how your savings have grown over time. This can be a huge motivator to keep saving and stay on track.

Gamify Saving

There are also apps that gamify the savings process, turning it into a fun challenge. For example, the app Digit analyzes your spending habits and automatically transfers small amounts of money into your savings account when you can afford it. The app Qapital lets you set rules for your savings, like rounding up each purchase to the nearest dollar and saving the change.

Saving and Discipline

Picture this: You're standing at the crossroads of your financial destiny. On one path, you see the glittering temptations of instant gratification. On the other, you see the steady, reliable route of saving – not as flashy, but it leads to a future of financial stability.

The choice is obvious... *but difficult!*

Choosing the path of saving takes real discipline. It's like being on a diet and walking past a donut shop. You know that sugary goodness is tempting, but sticking to your goals will pay off in the long run. And let's be real, watching your savings grow is just as sweet (*well, almost*).

Developing the discipline to save consistently is like building a muscle. At first, it might feel like a strain, but the more you flex that savings muscle, the stronger it becomes. Soon enough, saving will be as natural as brushing your teeth.

Delayed Gratification

There's always going to be a new shiny object vying for your attention and your hard-earned dollars. That's why you need to build the habit of *"delayed gratification"*. Here it is in action:

So you're walking through the mall, minding your own business, when suddenly, a shiny new gadget catches your eye. It's the iPhone 57, complete with a built-in espresso machine and a holographic display that projects your favorite memes. Your quivering hand involuntarily reaches for your wallet, ready to make it rain, but then you remember: *you're supposed to be saving for something more important.*

So, you take a deep breath, put on your best *"responsible near-adult"* face, and walk away from the sparkling iPhone 57. It's not easy; in fact, it very well may be one of the most difficult decisions you've made thus far in your young life, but you now understand that delayed gratification is the key to unlocking a better future.

So, the next time you're tempted to blow your cash on something frivolous, just remember: delayed gratification is your secret weapon. It might not be as exciting as buying a jetpack or a lifetime supply of gummy bears, but it's the financial equivalent of putting on your superhero cape and doing what's right.

Continue practicing delayed gratification, and you'll look back on many more moments like these and have thankful thoughts such as, *"Wow, I'm so glad I didn't buy that toaster that burns motivational quotes onto my bread."*

Build the habit

Another way to stay disciplined with saving is to make it a habit. Just like brushing your teeth or doing your homework, saving should become a regular part of your routine.

Set a schedule for when you'll transfer money into your savings account, and stick to it like glue. Whether it's every week, every paycheck, or every time you find a dollar in the laundry (*cha-ching!*), make saving a non-negotiable part of your financial plan.

At first, it might feel like a chore, but over time, saving will become second nature – something you do automatically without even thinking about it. You might even start to look forward to those regular transfers, watching your savings grow like a well-watered plant.

And if you ever feel your resolve wavering, just remember: every dollar you save is a step closer to your goals. Whether it's a new laptop, a down payment on a house, or maybe you're just really, *REALLY* set on the motivational quote toaster—your future self will thank you for the sacrifices you make now.

Accountability

It can also help to have an accountability partner on your savings journey. This could be a parent, sibling, or friend. Share your goals with your accountability partner and check in with each other regularly to stay motivated and on track. You can even make it a friendly competition—see who can save the most each month, with the winner getting bragging rights (*or maybe a small prize, like a homemade origami trophy crafted from dollar bills*).

Knowing that someone else is rooting for your success can be a powerful motivator to stay disciplined. When you're tempted to splurge on something you know good and well that you don't need, just picture your accountability partner's disapproving face. Plus, having someone to celebrate your wins with makes the whole savings process a lot more fun— who doesn't love a good high-five or happy dance?

So find yourself an accountability buddy and start saving together. With a little teamwork and a lot of determination, you'll be unstoppable in your quest for financial success!

ACTIVITY: Savings Goal Roadmap

Now, it's time to put your savings knowledge into action! Let's create a roadmap for one of your savings goals.

1. **Define Your Goal**: Choose what you're saving for. Define your goal using the SMART criteria: Specific, Measurable, Achievable, Relevant, and Time-bound.
2. **Set Monthly Milestones**: Decide how much money you need to save each month to meet your goal by your target date. Sketch out a timeline of these monthly savings amounts.
3. **Identify Challenges**: Think about possible obstacles, such as needing to cut back on expenses or upcoming events that might impact your savings. Plan ways to overcome these challenges.
4. **Incorporate Windfalls**: Factor in any expected extra money, like birthday money or those accidentally laundered dollar bills (*so fresh*), which could help boost your savings ahead of schedule.
5. **Commit and Motivate**: Write down why this goal matters to you and what achieving it would mean. Place your roadmap where you can see it daily to keep motivated.
6. **Review and Adjust**: Remember, your roadmap can change as needed. Update your plans as you progress to stay on track toward your goal.

Remember, this roadmap is a living document. As you progress on your savings journey, feel free to adjust your timeline, tactics, or even your goal as needed. The key is to stay flexible, stay focused, and keep moving forward.

Chapter 5

Smart Spending

The bitterness of poor quality remains long after the sweetness of low price is forgotten. —Benjamin Franklin

Imagine this: you've just received your first paycheck from your part-time job, and you're feeling pretty good about yourself. You've worked hard, and now you have some cold-hard cash to call your own. You might be tempted to celebrate by buying those limited-edition sneakers you've been eyeing or treating your friends to a gourmet pizza party, *but hold on there, moneybags!*

You see, many people fall victim to the siren song of frivolous spending. It's like their feelings hijack their wallet and go on a wild shopping spree without inviting their brain along for the ride. In the next section, we'll dive into some of the most common emotional triggers that can lead you to overspend so that you can learn to stay grounded and in control of your finances.

The Psychology Behind Spending

Have you ever found yourself browsing online shopping sites when you're feeling stressed or down, only to end up with a cart full of items you don't really need? Or have you ever gone out with friends and felt pressured to keep up with their spending habits, even if it means stretching your budget too thin?

If you answered yes to either of these questions, don't worry—you're not alone. In fact, there are a variety of psychological triggers that can lead us to make impulsive or emotional spending decisions, even when we know better.

Emotional Spending

One common trigger is emotional spending. When we're feeling stressed, anxious, or down, it's easy to turn to "*retail therapy*" as a way to cope. That new pair of shoes or the latest gadget might give us a temporary boost of happiness, but it's often short-lived and can lead to feelings of guilt or regret later on.

The thing is, emotional spending is totally normal, and we all do it from time to time. The key is to recognize when it's happening and find healthier ways to cope with those feelings. Instead of turning to spending, try calling up a friend to vent, going for a run to clear your head, or busting out your favorite hobby to get your mind off things. Your wallet will thank you and you'll feel better knowing that your money is going to more productive uses.

Social Pressures

Another big influence on our spending habits is social pressure. It's like there's this unspoken competition to see who can have the coolest stuff, the most epic experiences, and the most Insta-worthy moments. And when you're constantly bombarded with images of your peers rocking designer labels, jetting off on lavish vacations, and brunching at the trendiest spots in town, it's hard not to feel like you're missing out if you're not keeping up.

If you find yourself feeling pressured to spend beyond your means due to social influences, try taking a step back and reassessing your priorities. Unfollow accounts that make you feel like you're not measuring up, and seek out content that inspires you to live your best life within your means. Surround yourself with friends who support your financial goals and share your values, rather than those who constantly encourage you to spend, spend, spend.

Remember: true happiness and fulfillment come from living a life that's authentic to you, not from keeping up with someone else's highlight reel. So stay true to yourself, spend wisely, and don't let social pressure derail your financial journey.

Breaking the habit

So, how can we combat these psychological triggers and take control of our spending habits? The first step is simply being aware of them. When you find yourself feeling the urge to make an impulsive purchase, take a moment to pause and ask yourself what's really driving that desire. Are you buying something because you really need it, or because you're trying to fill an emotional void or keep up with someone else's lifestyle?

Another helpful strategy is to create a personal reward system that encourage saving over spending. For example, let's say you have a goal to save $500 over the next few months. Every time you resist the urge to make an unnecessary purchase and instead put that money towards your savings goal, give yourself a small reward, like watching an episode of your favorite show or treating yourself to a homemade dessert. Over time, these small rewards can help reinforce positive spending habits and make saving money feel more enjoyable and satisfying.

Evaluating Needs vs. Wants

In the grand scheme of personal finance, there's a vital skill that every savvy spender must master: the art of distinguishing between essential needs and discretionary wants. It's a battle as old as time itself – or at least as old as the first caveman who had to choose between a new club for hunting and a fancy painting for his cave wall.

In today's world, we're constantly bombarded with advertisements and messages telling us that we absolutely must have the latest and greatest products. From smartphones that can do everything but wash dishes to designer clothes that cost more than a month's rent, it's easy to get caught up in the whirlwind of consumerism.

But here's the thing: *learning to separate what we truly need from what we simply want in the moment is crucial for maintaining financial stability.*

When you're faced with a purchasing decision, take a step back and ask yourself: is this something I genuinely need, or is it just a fleeting desire? Will this purchase contribute to my long-term goals, or is it just a temporary rush of retail therapy?

Now, this doesn't mean you have to live like a monk and deny yourself all of life's little pleasures. Treating yourself occasionally is perfectly fine – after all, what's the point of working hard if you can't enjoy the fruits of your labor? The key is finding a balance between necessary expenses and the occasional indulgence.

Think Longer Term

So, how can we get better at evaluating needs vs. wants? One helpful strategy is to consider the difference between immediate gratification and long-term satisfaction. That new video game or trendy outfit might give you a quick rush of excitement, but will it still bring you joy and fulfillment a month or a year from now?

On the flip side, spending money on things like education, experiences with loved ones, or investments in your future can lead to a deeper sense of satisfaction and well-being over time.

The 24 Hour Rule

Imagine that you're scrolling through your favorite online store when, suddenly, a shiny new gadget catches your eye. Your finger hovers mere millimeters over the "add to cart" button, ready to seal the deal...

But wait! Before you take the plunge, consider trying the 24 hour rule. This simple strategy involves giving yourself a full day to think over any non-essential purchases before pulling the trigger.

During this time, ask yourself:

Do I really need this item, or is it just a passing fancy?

How will this purchase fit into my overall financial goals?

Is there a more cost-effective alternative?

Often, you'll find that the initial excitement fades away over the course of a day, and you'll be able to make a more clear-headed decision about whether the purchase is truly worth it.

Mind Over Matter

Ultimately, the key to mastering needs vs. wants is to cultivate a mindset of mindful consumption. This means being intentional and thoughtful about the purchases you make and focusing on items that add real value and meaning to your life. It's not about depriving yourself of all pleasure or indulgence but rather being selective and deliberate about where you choose to spend your hard-earned money.

For example, let's say you're a passionate musician and you've been eyeing a new guitar for months. While a new instrument might seem like a "want" at first glance, if playing music is a core value and source of joy for you, investing in a quality guitar that will last for years could be seen as a worthwhile "need." On the other hand, if you're simply feeling the urge to buy the latest fashion trend or tech gadget because everyone else has it, that's likely a "want" that you can easily do without.

As you practice evaluating needs vs. wants, keep in mind that everyone's priorities and values are different. What might be an essential need for one person could be a frivolous want for another, and that's okay. The key is to get clear on what matters most to you and to use that as a guidepost for your spending decisions.

Cost-Benefit Analysis of Purchases

This might sound like a fancy business term, but really, it's just a way of weighing the pros and cons of a potential purchase to determine if it's truly worth it.

One key aspect of cost-benefit analysis is assessing value beyond just the price tag. It's easy to get caught up in looking for the cheapest option or the biggest discount, but sometimes, a higher-priced item can actually be a better value in the long run.

Real-world examples

For example, let's say you're in the market for a new backpack for school. You find one option that's really cheap, but it's made with flimsy materials and doesn't have a lot of storage space. On the other hand, you find a higher-quality backpack that costs more upfront, but it's made with durable materials, has plenty of pockets and compartments, and comes with a lifetime warranty. While the second option might be more expensive in the short term, it could end up being a better value over time because it will last longer and serve your needs better.

Here's a more complex example...

Let's say you're in the market for a new laptop. One option is a budget-friendly model with basic specs and minimal features. The other option is a more expensive, high-performance laptop from a reputable brand known for its durability, speed, and advanced features.

At first glance, the cheaper laptop might seem like the more attractive choice. However, when you consider factors like processing power, storage capacity, battery life, and overall build quality, the pricier option starts to look more appealing.

While the high-performance laptop comes with a higher upfront cost, its superior specs and features can provide significant benefits in the long run. Faster processing speeds and more RAM can save you time and frustration when running multiple programs or working on resource-intensive tasks. A larger, high-quality display can reduce eye strain and enhance your overall user experience. A more durable build can mean fewer repairs and a longer lifespan for your device.

Moreover, the more expensive laptop can open up more opportunities to earn money through online gigs and freelance work. With a reliable, high-performance device, you can take on remote jobs such as video editing, graphic design, or computer-aided drafting (CAD). The extra income earned through these activities can help offset the initial cost of the laptop and even provide a valuable return on your investment.

When you factor in these potential financial benefits alongside the laptop's superior performance and longevity, the cost-benefit analysis starts to favor the more expensive, high-quality option. While it may require a larger upfront investment, the long-term value provided by a top-tier laptop can make it the smarter choice for your needs and goals.

Lifetime Cost

Another important factor to consider in cost-benefit analysis is the lifetime cost of a purchase. This includes not just the upfront purchase price, but also any ongoing costs associated with owning and maintaining the item over time.

Here's an example of the lifetime costs involved in, not an item, but an animal — a cute little puppy. Even if you were to adopt this puppy for free from an animal shelter, there are still a boatload of lifetime costs to consider, such as:

- Basic necessities (food, toys, bedding, grooming supplies)
- Home repairs (from when Scruffy was "teething")
- Routine veterinary care (annual check-ups, vaccinations, preventive medications)
- Unexpected medical expenses (injuries, illnesses)
- Training and pet-sitting services (obedience classes, doggy daycare, boarding)
- Pet rent, deposits, and potential liability insurance
- Time investment for daily care and attention

That adorable, fluffy face might be hard to resist, but remember: those big, soulful eyes are silently pleading, *"Adopt me, and I promise to love you unconditionally... and also drain your wallet for the next 15 years or so".*

Opportunity Cost

Every dollar you have represents an opportunity. When you spend money on one thing, *you're also choosing not to spend it on something else.* It's important to weigh these trade-offs carefully and make sure you're allocating your money in a way that aligns with your priorities and goals.

The key is to weigh not only what you're gaining from buying something, but also consider what you could be missing out on by losing the purchasing power of those dollars.

For example, consider the decision to buy a brand new gaming console that costs $500. While the console promises many hours of entertainment, it's important to consider the opportunity costs associated with both the financial investment and the time spent playing. That $500 could instead be used to enroll in several high-quality courses that you could invest your time into for a permanent boost in your skillset and marketability.

Evaluating these alternatives helps ensure that your spending and time allocation align with long-term personal and professional growth goals. By understanding the opportunity cost, you can make more intentional and beneficial decisions.

Stretching Your Dollar Further

Level up your spending game and make your hard-earned cash go the extra mile. With a few smart shopping strategies up your sleeve, you'll be able to score the best deals, save some serious dough, and still get your hands on the stuff you need (*and maybe even a few things you want*). So, let's dive in and explore some tips and tricks for making your dollars go further.

Compare Prices Like a Pro

Never settle for the first price tag you see. With a little bit of sleuthing, you can often find the same item for a lower price elsewhere. Before you pull the trigger on a purchase, take a few minutes to shop around and compare prices from different retailers, both online and in-store. Don't forget to factor in any shipping costs or membership fees that might apply.

Pro Tip: Use price comparison websites or apps to make the process even easier. These handy tools do the legwork for you, scouring the internet for the best deals on the products you're looking for. Some popular options include Google Shopping, PriceGrabber, and ShopSavvy.

Coupon Clipping 2.0

Forget about scissors and the Sunday paper—couponing has gone digital! These days, you can find coupons and discount codes for just about anything with a quick online search. Before you make a purchase, always do a quick Google search for the retailer's name plus "*coupon code*" or "*promo code.*" More often than not, you'll uncover a treasure trove of deals just waiting to be applied to your order.

Another great way to snag coupons is by signing up for your favorite retailers' email newsletters or following them on social media. Many brands will send exclusive discounts and promotions directly to their subscribers or followers.

Pro Tip: Use a separate email address for these subscriptions to avoid cluttering up your primary inbox.

Sale Season Savvy

Timing is everything when it comes to scoring the best deals. Most retailers follow a fairly predictable sale schedule throughout the year, so it pays to be strategic about when you shop. For example, end-of-season sales are a great time to stock up on clothing and accessories for the following year.

Holiday weekends like Memorial Day, Labor Day, and Black Friday/Cyber Monday are also known for their deep discounts across a wide range of products.

Of course, it's not always possible (or practical) to put off purchases until the next big sale comes around. In those cases, keep an eye out for flash sales, daily deals, or clearance events that pop up throughout the year. Sign up for email alerts from your favorite retailers or follow deal-sharing websites like Slickdeals or Wirecutter to stay in the loop.

Second-Hand Steals

Who says you have to buy everything brand new? Shopping second-hand is a smart way to save big on everything from clothing and accessories to electronics and home goods. Check out local thrift stores, consignment shops, or online marketplaces like eBay, Poshmark, or Facebook Marketplace for gently used items at a fraction of their original price.

Not only is buying second-hand easier on your wallet, but it's also better for the environment. By giving pre-loved items a new home, you're helping to reduce waste and keep perfectly good products out of landfills. Talk about a win-win!

The Art of Negotiation

Believe it or not, prices aren't always set in stone. In some cases, you may be able to negotiate a lower price or score additional perks just by asking. This is especially true when shopping for big-ticket items like electronics, furniture, or appliances. If you're buying in-store, don't be afraid to ask the salesperson if they can offer any discounts or throw in free delivery or installation.

When shopping online, try reaching out to the retailer's customer service team via live chat or email to inquire about any current promotions or discounts that might not be advertised on their website. The worst they can say is no, but you might be surprised at how often a little friendly haggling can pay off.

The Bottom Line

At the end of the day, smart shopping is all about being a savvy consumer and making informed decisions with your money. By taking the time to compare prices, seek out deals and discounts, and think outside the (*brand new*) box, you can stretch your budget further and get more bang for your buck.

Just remember: at the end of the day, the best deal isn't always the cheapest one. It's important to balance price with factors like quality, durability, and overall value. That almost-free, well-worn, thrift store t-shirt might seem like a steal in the moment, but unless you're going for that "*post-apocalyptic*" look, it might be worth investing a little extra in a t-shirt that won't disintegrate at the mere sight of a washing machine. Trust me, your wallet (*and your dignity*) will thank you in the long run.

So, go forth and shop smart, my frugal friend! With these strategies in your arsenal, you'll be well on your way to becoming a master of the bargain hunt.

Activity: Spending Diary

Now that we've covered all these key concepts of smart spending, it's time to put them into practice! One of the best ways to get a handle on your spending habits is to keep a spending diary. This means writing down every single purchase you make, no matter how small or seemingly insignificant.

1. **Choose Your Tool**: Decide whether you'll use a physical notebook, a digital spreadsheet, or a budgeting app to record your expenses.
2. **Record Daily**: Every day for the next month, write down every purchase you make. Include the date, what you bought, how much it cost, and optionally, how the purchase made you feel or why you decided to buy it.
3. **Review Monthly**: At the end of the month, review your entries. Look for patterns or trends in your spending. Identify any emotional triggers or frequent impulse buys.
4. **Analyze and Plan**: Use your findings to pinpoint areas for improvement. Set specific, achievable goals for the next month, such as limiting dining out expenses or setting aside a fixed amount for savings.
5. **Stay Consistent**: Keep the diary going and adjust your goals as needed, using it as a tool to guide and improve your spending habits.

At the end of the month, take some time to review your spending diary and reflect on your habits. Look for patterns and trends—are there certain triggers or emotions that tend to drive your spending? Are there any areas where you're consistently overspending or making impulse purchases?

Use this information to identify opportunities for improvement and set some clear goals for yourself moving forward. Maybe you want to challenge yourself to stick to a certain budget for eating out next month, or to put a certain amount of money towards your savings goals each week. Whatever your goals are, use your spending diary as a tool to help you stay accountable and on track.

Chapter 6

Credit and Debt: A Double-Edged Sword

Too many people spend money they haven't earned, to buy things they don't want, to impress people they don't like. —Will Rogers

Credit is like a double-edged sword. When used wisely, it can help you achieve your goals and build a strong financial foundation. But when mismanaged, it can lead to a crushing burden of debt that can take years to overcome. That's why it's so important to gain an understanding of credit and debt as early as possible so that you can learn to wield its mighty power responsibly.

Understanding Credit

Before we get into the nitty-gritty of using credit, let's take a step back and understand how it works.

When you use credit, you're essentially borrowing money from a lender (like a bank or credit card company) with the promise to pay it back over time, usually with interest. The lender is taking a risk by trusting you to repay the money, so they charge interest as a way to compensate for that risk and make a profit.

It's like they're saying, "*Sure, we'll lend you the money, but we're not running a charity here. We expect to get paid for our troubles and then some!*" The interest is the price you pay for the convenience of using someone else's money.

Credit can be a useful tool when used responsibly, but it's important to understand that *it's not free money*. It's essentially a loan with strings attached, and those strings can quickly turn into a tangled web of debt if you're not careful. So, when you're swiping that credit card, just remember that every purchase is like a little "IOU" note that you're signing.

Types Of Credit

There are a few different types of credit you might encounter as a teenager or young adult:

- **Credit cards:** These are probably the most common form of credit. With a credit card, you're given a credit limit (the maximum amount you can borrow) and you can use the card to make purchases or withdraw cash. You'll need to make at least the minimum payment each month, and if you don't pay off your balance in full, you'll be charged interest on the remaining amount.
- **Student loans:** If you're planning to go to college, you might need to take out student loans to cover the cost of tuition, books, and living expenses. These loans can come from the government or private lenders, and

they usually have lower interest rates than other types of credit. However, they also come with a lot of responsibility – you'll need to start paying them back after you graduate, even if you're not making a lot of money yet.

- **Personal loans:** A personal loan is a lump sum of money that you borrow from a bank or credit union and pay back over a set period of time, usually with fixed monthly payments. These loans can be used for a variety of purposes, like consolidating debt, paying for a big purchase, or covering an emergency expense.

- **Mortgages:** Okay, so you're probably not in the market for a house just yet, but it's still good to know what a mortgage is since they're a big part of most people's financial lives. A mortgage is a loan used to buy a home, and it's usually paid back over 15-30 years. The house itself serves as collateral for the loan, which means if you don't make your payments, the lender can take possession of the house.

Key Credit Terms

No matter what type of credit you're using, there are a few key terms you should know:

- **Credit limit:** The maximum amount you can borrow on a credit card or line of credit.
- **Interest rate:** The percentage in interest that you'll be charged each month if you don't pay off your balance in full.

- **Minimum payment:** The smallest amount you're required to pay each month to keep your account in good standing.
- **Credit score:** A number that represents your creditworthiness and helps lenders decide whether to approve you for credit and at what interest rate.

We'll talk more about credit scores later in this chapter, but for now, just know that your credit score is like a grade for how well you manage credit. The higher your score, the better!

The Pros and Cons of Using Credit

On the positive side, credit can be a valuable financial tool that offers flexibility and opportunity. It allows individuals to make purchases or investments that might otherwise be out of reach. When used responsibly, credit can help build a strong credit history and score. A good credit standing can open doors to better financial products, terms, and even certain career or housing prospects.

However, credit also comes with significant risks and potential drawbacks. Overreliance on credit can lead to unmanageable debt, especially if spending habits are not kept in check or if unexpected financial challenges arise. It's almost like the credit card companies are saying, "*Hey, want to buy something you can't afford? No problem! Just use this little magic, plastic rectangle, and worry about the consequences later!*" Before you know it, you're sitting in your apartment, surrounded by things you bought on credit, wondering where all your money went. The worst part? Not only are you broke, but you also owe someone else money.

It's a balancing act. You want to enjoy the benefits of credit without falling into the trap of debt.

The Pros Of Using Credit:

- **Build your credit score:** By making on-time payments and keeping your balances low, you can demonstrate to lenders that you're a responsible borrower and improve your credit score over time.
- **Make large purchases:** Sometimes, you might need to make a big purchase that you can't afford to pay for all at once (like a car or a computer for school). Using credit can allow you to spread out the cost over time, making it more manageable.
- **Cover emergency expenses:** Life happens, and sometimes unexpected expenses pop up (like a car repair or a medical bill). Having a credit card or personal loan can give you a safety net to fall back on in these situations.
- **Earn rewards:** Some credit cards offer rewards programs where you can earn points, miles, or cash back on your purchases. If you use your card regularly and pay off your balance in full each month, these rewards can add up to significant savings over time.

The Cons Of Using Credit:

- **Debt:** If you don't stay on top of your payments or you borrow more than you can afford to pay back, you can quickly find yourself in debt. And the longer you carry a balance, the more interest you'll accrue, making it harder to get out of debt. Remember when we talked about *compound interest*? Well, carrying high-interest debt is the polar-opposite of it. It's like being stuck in quicksand—the more you struggle, the deeper you sink. Before you know it, you're up to your eyeballs in interest charges, and your minimum payments are barely making a dent.

- **Temptation to overspend:** When you have a credit card or line of credit, it can be tempting to spend more than you normally would. After all, you're not seeing the money come directly out of your bank account. But remember – just because you can borrow the money doesn't mean you should. It's important to stick to your budget and only spend what you can afford to pay back.
- **Fees:** Many credit cards come with annual fees, balance transfer fees, cash advance fees, and other hidden costs. If you're not careful, these fees can add up quickly and make your debt even harder to pay off.
- **Impact on your credit score:** If you miss payments, max out your credit cards, or default on your loans, it can have a serious negative impact on your credit score. This can make it harder to get approved for credit in the future, and you may end up paying higher interest rates as a result.

Credit is like a powerful tool in your financial toolbox—it can help you build a strong credit score, make important purchases, and navigate life's unexpected challenges. But like any tool, it's important to learn how to use it properly to avoid hurting yourself in the process.

The key is to educate yourself on responsible credit use, including paying your bills on time, keeping your balances low, and avoiding the temptation to overspend just because you have a shiny new credit card burning a hole in your pocket.

Building and Maintaining a Good Credit Score

Now that we've covered the basics of credit and debt, let's talk about the importance of building and maintaining a good credit score.

Your credit score is your financial report card – it reflects how well you manage credit and how risky you are as a borrower. Lenders use your credit score to decide whether to approve you for credit, and at what interest rate. Landlords, employers, and even cell phone companies may also use your credit score to make decisions about you.

So, how is your credit score calculated? There are a few key factors that go into it:

- **Payment history:** This is the most important factor in your credit score. It looks at whether you've made your payments on time, and if you have any late payments, collections, or defaults on your record.
- **Credit utilization:** This is how much of your available credit you're using at any given time. It's generally recommended to keep your credit utilization below 30% (so if you have a $1,000 credit limit, try to keep your balance below $300).
- **Length of credit history:** The longer you've been using credit, the better. This shows lenders that you have experience managing credit responsibly.

- **Types of credit:** Having a mix of different types of credit (like credit cards, student loans, and a car loan) can also help your score.
- **New credit inquiries:** Every time you apply for new credit, it results in a hard inquiry on your credit report. Too many hard inquiries in a short period of time can be a red flag to lenders.

So, how can you build and maintain a good credit score as a teenager or young adult? Here are a few tips:

1. **Start with a secured credit card or credit-builder loan:** If you're new to credit, you might have a hard time getting approved for a regular credit card. A secured credit card or credit-builder loan can help you build credit without taking on too much risk. With a secured card, you put down a cash deposit that serves as collateral for your credit limit. With a credit-builder loan, you borrow a small amount of money and make monthly payments, which are reported to the credit bureaus. It's an easy way to get the ball rolling.

2. **Use credit responsibly:** Once you have a credit card or loan, it's important to use it responsibly. Make your payments on time every month, and try to pay off your balance in full if possible. If you can't pay in full, at least make the minimum payment and work on paying down your balance over time.

3. **Monitor your credit report:** You're entitled to a free credit report from each of the three major credit bureaus (Equifax, Experian, and TransUnion) once a year. Take advantage of this and review your credit

report regularly for errors or signs of fraud. If you see anything suspicious, dispute it right away.

4. **Don't apply for too much credit at once:** Remember, every time you apply for credit, it results in a hard inquiry on your credit report. Too many of these can ding your score, so only apply for credit when you really need it.

5. **Be patient:** Building a good credit score takes time. It's not something that happens overnight, but with consistent, responsible credit use, you can gradually improve your score over time.

By following these tips and using credit responsibly, you'll be well on your way to building a strong credit foundation that will serve you well throughout your adult life.

The Dangers of Debt

While using credit responsibly can be a good thing, it's important to be aware of the dangers of debt. When you borrow money, you're committing to paying it back – with interest. And if you're not careful, that debt can quickly spiral out of control.

Here are a few common debt traps to watch out for:

- **High-interest credit cards:** Credit cards can be a convenient way to make purchases, but they often come with high interest rates (especially for people with lower credit scores). If you only make the minimum payment each month, you could end up paying a lot more in interest over time.

- **Payday loans:** These are short-term loans that are designed to be paid back on your next payday. They often come with extremely high interest rates and fees, which can make them very difficult to pay off. It's best to avoid payday loans altogether if possible.
- **Rent-to-own programs:** These programs allow you to rent items (like furniture or electronics) with the option to buy them at the end of the rental period. However, the total cost of the item usually ends up being much higher than if you had bought it outright, and you may end up paying a lot in fees and interest.
- **Overusing student loans:** While student loans can be a helpful way to pay for college, it's important to borrow only what you need. Taking out more loans than necessary can leave you with a lot of debt to pay back after graduation, which can be a big financial burden.

Avoiding The Debt-Trap

It's all too easy to fall into the trap of spending more than you can afford, only to find yourself drowning in a sea of minimum payments and interest charges. Before you know it, you're playing a game of financial whack-a-mole, trying to keep up with your bills while your credit score sinks faster than a submarine with screen doors.

So, how do you avoid this financial faux pas?

- **Live within your means:** Avoid spending more than you earn, and stick to a budget that allows you to save money each month.

- **Save up for big purchases:** Instead of relying on credit to make big purchases, try to save up the money in advance. This can help you avoid taking on debt and paying interest.
- **Use credit responsibly:** Only charge what you can afford to pay back, and make your payments on time each month.
- **Have an emergency fund:** Try to save up a small emergency fund (even just a few hundred dollars) that you can use to cover unexpected expenses. This can help you avoid turning to credit or loans in a pinch.
- **Seek help if you need it:** If you find yourself struggling with debt, don't be afraid to seek help. Talk to a financial advisor or credit counselor who can help you create a plan to pay off your debt and get back on track.

Remember, debt isn't always avoidable, nor should it be avoided outright. By being proactive and making smart financial choices, you can minimize your risk, keep your debt under control, and learn to wield credit like the helpful financial tool it's meant to be and avoid treating it like a bottomless piggybank.

ACTIVITY: Credit & Debt Quiz

Test your knowledge concerning the important topic of "Credit & Debt" by taking a quick, 8-question quiz:

1. What is credit? a) Money you have in your bank account b) The ability to borrow money with the promise to pay it back later, often with interest c) A

gift card for your favorite store d) A type of currency used in foreign countries

2. Which of the following is NOT a type of credit? a) Credit cards b) Student loans c) Amazon Gift Cards d) Payday loans

3. What does a credit score represent? a) The amount of money you have in your savings account b) Your creditworthiness and how risky you are as a borrower c) The number of credit cards you own d) Your monthly income

4. Which factor is most important in determining your credit score? a) Payment history b) Length of credit history c) Types of credit d) New credit inquiries

5. What is the recommended credit utilization percentage to maintain a good credit score? a) 50% b) 75% c) 30% d) 90%

6. How often are you entitled to a free credit report from each of the three major credit bureaus? a) Once a month b) Once a year c) Every two years d) Never

7. Which of the following is NOT a good tip for avoiding debt? a) Living within your means b) Saving up for big purchases c) Using credit responsibly d) Taking out the largest loans possible.

8. If you're struggling with debt, what should you do? a) Ignore the problem and hope it goes away b) Take out more loans to pay off your existing debt c) Seek help from a financial advisor or credit counselor d) Cut up all your credit cards and never use them again

Answer Key: 1b, 2c, 3b, 4a, 5c, 6b, 7d, 8c

Chapter 7

Your Voice Matters

We rise by lifting others. — Robert Ingersoll

You're more than halfway through this journey of learning how to manage your money and take control of your financial future. Give yourself a well-deserved pat on the back for making it this far!

As you've been reading, you've probably had a few *"aha!"* moments.

Wouldn't it be amazing if you could share those moments with other teens and help them experience the same kind of financial empowerment?

By leaving a review of this book on Amazon, you're not just helping other teens – you're stepping up as an advocate for smart money management.

Simply scan the QR code and leave your review:

It only takes a minute, but your review can make a huge difference.

Your words have the power to change lives – and that's an incredible thing!

You're biggest fan,

Ben Clardy

Now, let's get back into the book!

Chapter 8
Investing 101

Know what you own, and know why you own it.
—Peter Lynch

Investing is one of the most powerful tools you have for building long-term wealth and creating the life you want. Also, anyone can start investing, no matter how much cash you have or how little you know about the stock market!

Most people think that the #1 goal of investing is to *"get rich"*, but that's entirely wrong. *What it's really about is giving yourself options and freedom.* It's about being able to afford the things that matter to you—whether that's traveling the world, starting your own business, or being able to help out your family. And the earlier you start investing, the more time you have for your money to grow.

Buying Assets

First things first, let's break down what investing actually means. Basically, investing is all about putting your money into an asset (like stocks, bonds, real estate, gold, etc.) with the expectation of that asset increasing in value over time. In other words, instead of just letting your cash sit around doing nothing, you're putting it to work so it can grow.

When you invest, you're basically becoming the owner or part-owner of whatever you're investing in. So, if you buy a stock, congrats—you own a tiny piece of that company! And if that company makes money and grows, the value of your stock goes up, too. Sometimes, the company might even send you a slice of their profits just for being an owner—that's called a dividend.

But here's the thing—investing is not a get-rich-quick scheme. It's a long-term game that requires patience and discipline. There will be times when your investments go up in value and times when they go down. That's just part of the ride. The key is to stay focused on your big-picture goals and not get too caught up in the day-to-day ups and downs.

Ways To invest

Picture yourself strolling down the aisles of a financial supermarket, where the shelves are lined with a dizzying array of investment products. Each one promises to be the key to unlocking your financial dreams, like a shiny new toy begging to be taken home. But before you start tossing random investments into your cart like a kid in a candy store, it's important to take a step back and consider your options.

The point is—there's no one-size-fits-all approach to investing. What works for your neighbor or your second cousin twice removed might not be the right fit for you. It's all about figuring out your own financial recipe based on your goals, risk tolerance, and personal taste.

Here's an overview of the basic investment types:

Stocks

You've probably seen it in the movies—the intense stock trader, eyes glued to a wall of computer screens filled with charts and numbers, frantically making deals and watching their fortune grow (or disappear) with each passing second. While the reality of stock trading may not be quite as dramatic, it's true that investing in stocks can be an exciting and potentially lucrative way to grow your wealth over time.

When you buy a stock, you're buying a piece of ownership in a company. It's like becoming a mini-mogul, without the private jet and the corner office. Plus, some companies even pay dividends to their shareholders, which is like getting a little bonus check just for being an owner.

One thing to keep in mind about stocks is that they can be quite unpredictable. They have their moments of exhilarating growth, but they can also take sudden dives that might leave you feeling uneasy. Much like navigating a stormy sea, the key is to remain steady and not let your emotions steer the ship. If you can maintain your composure through these ups and downs, stocks can be a potent tool for building wealth over time.

Bonds

When you buy a bond, you're basically lending money to a company or government. It's like being a bank but without the stuffy suits and the free lollipops. The borrower promises to pay you back the original amount (called the principal) plus interest over a set period of time, usually several years. It's like you lend someone some money, and they give you back an IOU, but with a little extra *somethin' somethin'* on top.

Bonds are generally less risky than stocks because you know exactly how much you'll get back and when. They're like the slow and steady tortoise to the stock market's manic hare. But that doesn't mean they're completely risk-free. If the borrower defaults on their payments, you could be left holding the bag (a bag that used to contain money *but no longer does*). This doesn't happen often, but it's a possibility. Still, for investors who want a little more stability in their portfolio, bonds can be a solid choice.

Mutual Funds and ETFs

These are like baskets of investments that can include stocks, bonds, and other assets all mixed together. It's like going to an all-you-can-eat buffet and getting a big plate with a little bit of everything piled on it. When you invest in a fund, you're pooling your money with other investors to buy a mix of different investments, which can help spread out your risk.

The beauty of mutual funds and ETFs (Exchange-Traded Funds) is that you don't have to be a financial whiz to invest in them. You don't have to spend hours pouring over stock charts or analyzing bond yields—the fund managers do all the heavy lifting for you. It's like having a personal chef for your investments, minus the fancy hat and the French accent. Of course, you'll pay a fee for their services, but for many investors, it's worth it for the convenience and peace of mind.

Index Funds

Imagine you're at a gigantic farmers market. Instead of spending hours examining every apple, carrot, and head of lettuce, you simply buy a small piece of every single stand. That's essentially what an index fund does in the world of investing.

Index funds are the cool, laid-back cousin of mutual funds and ETFs. They're like the reliable family car of the investment world—not flashy, but dependable and gets you where you need to go without emptying your wallet. It's as if someone took a snapshot of the entire market (or a big chunk of it) and turned it into one easy-to-buy package.

Consider Vanguard to be your go-to company for investing in index funds. Vanguard is like the pioneer of index funds. They've been doing this longer than anyone else and they're known for keeping costs super low, which means more money stays in your pocket.

So, why are investors head over heels for index funds?

- **They're cheap to own:** Index funds typically have lower fees than actively managed funds. They don't need a team of suit-wearing analysts trying to outsmart the market.
- **They play the field:** By tracking an entire index, you're instantly diversified across hundreds or even thousands of companies. It's like going to a buffet and tasting a little bit of everything.

- **They're low maintenance:** You don't need to pick individual stocks or time the market. Just buy the index and hold on for the long term. It's perfect for those who'd rather spend their time binge-watching their favorite shows than poring over financial statements.
- **They've got street cred:** Over long periods, index funds have often outperformed actively managed funds, especially after accounting for fees. It's like they've cracked the code of the investing universe.

For many investors, especially beginners, index funds offer an easy, low-cost way to get started with investing. They're like the "set it and forget it" option of the investment world. So, if you're looking for a simple, cost-effective way to dip your toes into the investing pool, index funds might just be your new best friend.

Real Estate

Buying real estate directly is like playing a high-stakes game of Monopoly, except with real cash and actual buildings. It's not for the faint of heart, but if you've got the guts and the capital, it can be a rewarding way to invest. Just be prepared to deal with the occasional leaky roof, problem tenant, and 2 a.m. phone call about a clogged toilet. It's all part of the charm of owning real estate.

If you're not quite ready to go all-in on the property ownership game, a real estate Investment Trust (REIT) can be a more accessible way to dip your toes into the real estate pool. REITs are like the mutual funds of the real estate world. They own and manage a portfolio of properties, and you can buy shares in the trust just like you would with a stock. They come in all shapes and sizes, from residential to commercial, and offer a way to invest in real estate without the massive capital outlay and hands-on management that comes with buying property directly. Plus, they typically offer higher returns than many other types of investments.

Cryptocurrencies

Cryptocurrencies like Bitcoin and Ethereum have been stealing the spotlight lately. Known for their roller coaster-like volatility, these digital currencies can make your financial portfolio feel a bit like a daring adventure at an amusement park.

When considering whether to invite Bitcoin or Ethereum to your investment party, it's wise to start with a solid foundation of traditional investments tailored to your financial goals and risk appetite. Think of it as enjoying a sturdy, balanced meal before indulging in dessert. This mix might include stocks, bonds, mutual funds, and perhaps some real estate—a bit less exciting but reliably nourishing over the long term.

As your confidence and knowledge expand, feel free to spice up your portfolio with a sprinkle of cryptocurrencies. Just remember that while they can add a dash of excitement and the potential for big returns, they can be quite risky.

Risk vs. Reward

One of the core concepts to understand about investing is the relationship between risk and reward. In general, investments that have the potential to earn more money also come with a higher degree of risk, AKA: *losing money*. On the flip side, investments that are less risky usually have lower potential returns. They might not make you rich quickly, but they can provide steadier and more predictable yields.

Weighing Risk

So, how much risk should you take? That depends on your goals and timeline. If you have the time, money, and stomach to ride out the ups and downs of the market, you might be comfortable taking on more risk for the potential of higher returns. But if you're saving up for a short-term goal (like buying a car or paying for college), you might want to play it a bit safer.

One way to think about risk is to imagine a spectrum, with low-risk investments (like bonds) on one end and high-risk investments (like some stocks or cryptocurrencies) on the other end. Most people's portfolios will fall somewhere in the middle, with a mix of different types of investments.

Protect the eggs

Another way to manage risk is through diversification— affectionately known in financial circles as *not putting all your eggs in one basket.*

Imagine you're a farmer with a thriving egg business. You've got a flock of hens that lay delicious, fresh eggs every day, and you rely on those eggs for your livelihood. Now, picture yourself collecting all those eggs and carefully stacking them up into a single basket.

Risky move, isn't it? All it takes is one little stumble and you've got the makings of the world's largest omelet.

When you concentrate all your resources into a single venture, you leave yourself vulnerable to potential catastrophes. If that one investment fails, your entire financial future could be jeopardized.

The solution? *Diversification.*

Just as a wise farmer would distribute their eggs across multiple baskets to mitigate risk, a savvy investor will spread their money across various assets. This way, if one investment underperforms or faces a setback, the overall impact on your portfolio is minimized. Your other investments can help cushion the blow and keep you on track toward your financial goals.

Of course, diversification isn't a magic bullet. It can't entirely eliminate risk, and it's still possible to experience losses even in a well-diversified portfolio. However, by embracing the principle of not putting all your eggs in one basket, you can significantly reduce your exposure to potential disasters and increase your chances of weathering any financial storms that come your way.

Building Your Portfolio

Okay, so you know the basics of investing and the different types of investments out there. But how do you actually put it all together into a portfolio that works for you? That's where asset allocation comes in.

Asset allocation is just a fancy way of saying, "*deciding how much of your money to put into different types of investments.*"

A common approach is to decide on a mix of stocks, bonds, and other assets based on your age, goals, and risk tolerance.

For example, let's say you're 16 years old and you're investing for the long haul (like retirement). You might start with a portfolio that looks something like this:

- 70% stocks (for long-term growth potential)
- 25% bonds (for stability and income)
- 5% cash/short-term investments (for short-term goals)

As you get older and closer to needing your money, you might start shifting more of your portfolio into bonds and cash to reduce your risk. So, by the time you're in your 60s, your portfolio might look more like this:

- 50% stocks
- 40% bonds
- 10% cash/short-term investments

Of course, these are just examples—your actual asset allocation will depend on your specific goals and circumstances. As you learn more about investing, you might decide to add other types of investments to your portfolio, like real estate or crypto.

Putting Your Investing Plan into Action

Now that you've got a solid understanding of the different types of investments and how to craft a portfolio that aligns with your financial goals and risk tolerance, you might be itching to dive right in and start putting your money to work. But hold up! If you're not quite 18 yet, you'll need to get a parent or guardian involved to officially start investing. Think of it like getting your learner's permit before you can officially hit the road solo.

Here's a step-by-step guide to getting started:

1. **Set your goals:** Before you start investing, it's important to know what you're investing for. Are you saving up for a big purchase (like a car or a house down payment)? Investing for retirement? Building an emergency fund? Write down your goals and how much money you'll need to reach them.

2. **Open an account:** If you're under 18, you'll need a parent or guardian to open an account on your behalf. You'll be looking for a "Custodial Account" or a "Joint Brokerage Account". Once you are 18, you can have your own account. Look for an account with low fees and a good selection of investment options.

3. **Decide on your asset allocation:** Based on your goals and risk tolerance, decide how you want to split your money between stocks, bonds, and other investments.

4. **Choose your investments:** Once you've decided on your asset allocation, it's time to pick your specific investments. Look for low-cost index funds or ETFs that give you broad exposure to different parts of the stock and bond markets. As you learn more, you can start adding individual stocks or other types of investments to your portfolio.

5. **Set up automatic contributions:** To make investing a habit, set up automatic transfers from your bank account into your investment account. Start with whatever amount you can afford (even $10 or $20 a week can really add up over time!), and increase your contributions as your income grows.

6. **Monitor and rebalance:** As your investments grow (or shrink) over time, your asset allocation might start to drift away from your target. For example, if your stocks do really well, they might start to take up a bigger chunk of your portfolio than you originally planned. To keep things on track, check in on your portfolio a few times a year and rebalance as needed.

Teen Investors Who Are Crushing It

Still not convinced that investing is for you? Check out these real-life stories of teens who are making big things happen:

- **Saahil, 19:** Saahil started investing when he was just 16 years old, using money he earned from tutoring and freelance web design. He started with a mix of index funds and individual stocks, and has already grown his portfolio to over $7,000. "*Investing has taught me so much about how the world works,*" Saahil says. "*It's not just about making money—it's about understanding business and even the global economy.*"

- **Maya, 16:** Maya got interested in investing after taking a personal finance class at her high school. She started by investing $50 a month from her part-time job, and has slowly built up a diversified portfolio of stocks and bonds. "*I love watching my investments grow*," Maya says. "It's *like planting a seed and watching it turn into a huge tree.*"

- **Jamal, 15:** With the aid of his Grandpa, Jamal went an entirely different route. Instead of buying stocks, he buys rare gold and silver coins. He started off by purchasing an American Gold Eagle coin with the money he saved from birthdays and allowance—and a little help from his Grandpa. While the value of gold can fluctuate in the short term, Jamal understands that precious metals have historically been a reliable store of value over long periods. He plans to gradually expand his collection, focusing on high-quality, rare coins that have the potential to grow in value due to their scarcity and historical significance.

Investing Myths: Busted!

I know we've talked about a lot in this chapter, so before we wrap it up, let's bust some common myths about investing that might be holding you back:

- **Myth #1:** You need a lot of money to start investing. Not true! You can start investing with just $5 a week — or even less! The amount isn't nearly as important as starting early and being consistent.
- **Myth #2:** Investing is too risky. While all investments come with some level of risk, there are ways to manage that risk through diversification and asset allocation. Historically, the stock market has actually been one of the best ways to grow your wealth over the long term.

- **Myth #3:** Investing is only for old people. No way! In fact, the earlier you start investing, the more time you have to let your money grow and compound over time. So don't wait—start investing as young as possible!

ACTIVITY: Practice Trading Account

Ready to put your investing knowledge into action? Let's set up a practice investment account and get some hands-on experience with the market. This is an excellent way to get very real experience, but without risking any real money.

Setting Up Your Practice Account

1. **Choose a stock market simulator:** There are lots of free options out there, like Investopedia's Stock Simulator, Wall Street Survivor, or HowTheMarketWorks. These simulators let you practice investing with virtual money, so you can learn the ropes without risking any real cash.
2. **Create an account:** Once you've picked a simulator, sign up for an account. You'll usually need to provide some basic info like your name and email address, and also create a username and password. It's best to have a parent help with this.
3. **Explore the platform:** Take some time to familiarize yourself with the simulator's interface. Look for things like your account balance, the stock search function, and any educational resources or tutorials.
4. **Fund your account:** Most simulators will give you a set amount of virtual cash to start with (like

$100,000). This is your risk-free "play money" to invest in the stock market.

Building Your Practice Portfolio

1. **Set some goals:** Before you start investing, take a minute to think about what you want to achieve. Are you trying to grow your money as much as possible? Learn about a specific industry or type of investment? Manage risk? Write down your goals so you can refer back to them as you build your portfolio.
2. **Do your research:** Use the simulator's stock search function to look up companies you're interested in. Read through their financial statements, news articles, and analyst reports to get a sense of their business and growth prospects.
3. **Make your first trades:** When you're ready, place your first virtual trades! Most simulators will let you buy and sell stocks, bonds, ETFs, and other investments just like you would with a real brokerage account.
4. **Monitor your progress:** Keep an eye on how your investments are doing over time. Most simulators will give you real-time stock quotes and portfolio performance data. Use this info to track your returns, spot trends, and make adjustments as needed.

Learning from Your Practice Trades

- **Reflect on your strategy:** As you build your practice portfolio, take some time to reflect on your investment strategy. What's working well? What could you improve? Are you taking on too much (or too little) risk?

- **Learn from your mistakes:** Everyone makes mistakes when they're learning to invest—that's part of the process! If a trade doesn't go your way, don't beat yourself up. Instead, try to learn from the experience and use that knowledge to make better decisions next time.
- **Keep learning:** The stock market is always changing, so it's important to keep learning and staying up-to-date. Read investing books and articles, follow financial news, and talk to other investors to keep expanding your knowledge.
- **Have fun:** Investing can be serious business—but it can also be a lot of fun! Enjoy the thrill of watching your virtual portfolio grow, and don't be afraid to take some calculated risks. Remember, this is all practice—so have fun and keep learning!

Chapter 9
Protecting Your Money

If you don't protect your money, you will have no means to protect anything else in your life.
—Tony Robbins

So far, you've learned about the importance of budgeting, saving, making smart spending decisions, and even ways of investing your hard-earned cash. But there's one more crucial aspect of financial literacy that we need to discuss: *protecting your money.*

In today's digital age, financial security is more important than ever. From identity theft to online scams, there are countless threats out there that can put your financial well-being at risk.

But don't worry—by arming yourself with the right knowledge and tools, you can keep your money safe and secure. In this chapter, we'll dive into the basics of financial security, including how to protect yourself from identity theft, stay safe while banking online, and safeguard your digital footprint.

Basics of Financial Security

First things first, let's talk about the fundamentals of financial security. It's about being proactive in managing your finances and taking steps to ensure that your money is always safe and secure.

Financial Audit

One of the most important aspects of financial security is regularly conducting audits. This means taking the time to review your personal financial statements and accounts, looking for any unauthorized transactions or discrepancies. It might sound tedious, but trust me—it's worth it. By catching any suspicious activity early on, you can prevent small issues from turning into very big problems down the line.

To conduct a financial audit, start by gathering all of your financial statements, including bank statements, credit card bills, and investment account statements. Review each transaction carefully, looking for any charges or withdrawals that you don't recognize. If you spot anything suspicious, contact your financial institution immediately to report the issue and take steps to resolve it.

Here are some specific steps you can take to conduct a thorough financial audit:

1. Make a list of all your financial accounts, including bank accounts, credit cards, investment accounts, and any other accounts that hold your money.
2. Gather all relevant statements and documents for each account, going back at least a few months.

3. Review each transaction on your statements, checking for any unfamiliar or unauthorized charges.
4. Pay particular attention to small, recurring charges that you might have forgotten about, such as subscriptions or membership fees.
5. If you find any suspicious activity, contact the relevant financial institution immediately to report the issue and start the process of recovering any lost funds.
6. Consider using budgeting apps or software to help you keep track of your spending and spot any unusual activity more easily.

Document Storage

Another key aspect of financial security is secure document storage. This means keeping all of your important financial documents, such as bank statements, tax returns, and investment account statements, in a safe and secure location. Ideally, you should store physical documents in a fireproof safe or lockbox, and keep digital copies in an encrypted storage solution, such as a password-protected cloud storage account.

Back It Up

Picture this: you've been diligently tracking your budget, saving for your future, and maybe even planning a side hustle to boost your income. All your important financial documents are neatly organized on your computer. But what happens if your trusty laptop decides to take an early retirement, gets stolen, or simply crashes without warning? All of your hard work could disappear in an instant.

That's where the smart habit of regularly backing up your crucial financial files comes in handy. By copying your documents to an external hard drive or a secure cloud storage service, you're essentially creating a safety net for your financial records.

Imagine the relief you'll feel when you can quickly access your backup files and carry on with your financial plans without missing a beat. After all, it's better to be safe than sorry—especially when "sorry" involves trying to recreate lost financial documents while sobbing over a tear-soaked keyboard.

Scams

It's also crucial to stay alert and informed about common financial scams and frauds to avoid falling victim to them. Scammers are like modern-day pirates, always on the lookout for their next unsuspecting victim.

Staying one step ahead means questioning anything that sounds too good to be true, guarding your personal information like it's the secret formula for Coca-Cola, and remembering that even the most convincing con artists can't guarantee you a quick fortune.

Being informed and skeptical is your best defense—because when it comes to your finances, it's always better to trust your gut than let an unsolicited scam email convince you of being the rightful heir to the vast fortune of a recently departed Arabian Prince.

Speaking of scams, here are some different types:

- **Phishing scams:** These are fake emails or messages that appear to be from legitimate companies or institutions, often asking you to click on a link or provide personal information. Be very cautious about unsolicited messages, and always verify the sender before taking any action.
- **Romance scams:** These often start on dating apps or social media, with scammers building a fake relationship with their target before asking for money to help with an emergency or to come visit. Be wary of anyone you meet online who asks for money, no matter how convincing their story may seem.
- **Employment scams:** These often involve fake job postings, or unsolicited job offers that require you to pay for training or supplies upfront. Legitimate employers will never ask you to pay to start a job.
- **Cryptocurrency scams:** With the rise of cryptocurrencies like Bitcoin, there has also been an increase in related scams, such as fake investment opportunities or "pump and dump" schemes. Be very cautious about any crypto-related investments and always do your own research before putting any money in.

By being aware of these common scams and taking steps to protect your financial information, you can greatly reduce your risk of falling victim to financial fraud. Remember, if something seems too good to be true, it probably is!

Identity Theft Protection

One of the biggest threats to financial security in today's digital age is identity theft. Identity theft occurs when someone steals your personal information, such as your Social Security number or credit card details, and uses it to open fraudulent accounts or make unauthorized purchases in your name. It can be a nightmare to deal with, often taking months or even years to recover from fully.

The good news is that there are steps you can take to protect yourself from identity theft. One of the most important things you can do is regularly monitor your credit reports from the three major credit bureaus: Equifax, Experian, and TransUnion. Your credit report contains a detailed history of your credit accounts and payment history and is often the first place where signs of identity theft will appear.

Credit Report Check

By law, you are entitled to one free credit report from each bureau every year. You can request your reports online at AnnualCreditReport.com, or by calling 1-877-322-8228. Review your reports carefully, looking for any accounts or inquiries that you don't recognize. If you spot anything suspicious, contact the credit bureau immediately to dispute the information and place a fraud alert on your account.

Freeze!

Another way to protect yourself is by placing a credit freeze on your accounts. A credit freeze restricts access to your credit report, making it much harder for identity thieves to open new accounts in your name. To place a freeze, you'll need to contact each credit bureau individually and provide proof of your identity. You can lift the freeze at any time if you need to apply for new credit, but it provides an extra layer of security when you don't.

Keep it Personal

Another important aspect of identity theft protection is securing your personal information. This means being cautious about sharing sensitive details, such as your Social Security number or bank account information, especially online or over the phone. It also means taking steps to physically secure your personal documents, such as shredding sensitive papers before throwing them away and using complex passwords for all of your online accounts.

High Security

I'm ashamed to admit it, but once upon a time I actually used the password *"PASSWORD"*, for my email account. Not the smartest decision concerning my personal security, but I've learned a lot since then.

Now my password is:

NvrGnnaGvUup_NvrGnnaLtUdown_1987!

(Not really, but that's a pretty good one, right?)

When creating passwords, it's important to use a combination of upper and lowercase letters, numbers, and special characters. Avoid using easily guessable information like your birthdate or pet's name, and never use the same password for multiple accounts. Consider using a password manager to help you generate and store strong, unique passwords for all of your accounts.

Damage Control

If you do suspect that your identity has been stolen, it's important to act quickly to minimize the damage. Here are some steps to take:

1. Contact the credit bureaus to place a fraud alert on your account. This will make it harder for anyone to open new accounts in your name.
2. Report the theft to the Federal Trade Commission (FTC) at IdentityTheft.gov. The FTC can help you create a recovery plan and provide additional resources and support.
3. Contact any creditors or financial institutions where you believe fraudulent activity has occurred. Close any compromised accounts and request new account numbers and passwords.
4. Consider placing a credit freeze on your accounts, which will prevent anyone from opening new accounts in your name without your explicit permission.
5. File a report with your local police department, especially if you have evidence of the theft or know the identity of the thief.
6. Keep detailed records of all correspondence related to the theft, including dates, names, and contact information. This will be important if you need to dispute any fraudulent activity or take legal action.

Remember, recovering from identity theft can be a long and

difficult process, but staying vigilant and taking quick action can help minimize the damage and get you back on track.

Online Banking Safety

In today's digital age, online banking has become a convenient and essential tool for managing our finances. But with the convenience of online banking also comes the risk of cyber threats and scams. To keep your money safe while banking online, it's important to follow some key best practices.

Two Factor Authentification

One of the most important things you can do to secure your online banking accounts is to enable two-factor authentication (2FA). 2FA adds an extra layer of security beyond just a password, typically by requiring you to enter a one-time code sent to your phone or email whenever you log in to your account. This makes it much harder for hackers to gain unauthorized access to your accounts, even if they manage to steal your password.

Most major banks and financial institutions offer 2FA as an optional security feature, so be sure to enable it on all of your accounts. It may take a few extra seconds to log in each time, but the added security is well worth the minor inconvenience.

When setting up 2FA, be sure to use a phone number or email address that only you have access to. Avoid using shared or public accounts, as this could compromise the security of your 2FA codes.

In addition to enabling 2FA, it's also important to use strong, unique passwords for all of your online banking accounts. Avoid using easily guessable information like your birthdate or address, and never use the same password for multiple accounts. Consider using a password manager to help you generate and store complex passwords securely.

Public Wi-Fi

It's also important to be cautious about conducting financial transactions over unsecured or public Wi-Fi networks. These networks are often unencrypted, meaning that anyone nearby can potentially intercept your data and steal your sensitive information. Whenever possible, conduct online banking and other financial transactions over a secure, private network, such as your home Wi-Fi or a virtual private network (VPN).

If you do need to access your online banking accounts while on the go, be sure to use your cellular data connection instead of public Wi-Fi. You can also use a VPN app to encrypt your data and protect your privacy, even on public networks.

By following these best practices and staying vigilant about potential threats, you can enjoy the convenience of online banking while keeping your money safe and secure.

Protecting Your Digital Footprint

In addition to securing your online banking accounts, it's important to protect your overall digital footprint to maintain your financial security. Your digital footprint includes all of the information about you that exists online, from your social media profiles to your search history and online purchases. If this information falls into the wrong hands, it can be used to steal your identity, access your financial accounts, or worse.

One of the best ways to protect your digital footprint is to be mindful of your privacy settings and permissions on social media and other online accounts. Take the time to review your settings regularly, and make sure that you're only sharing information with trusted friends and contacts. Be especially cautious about sharing financial information online, such as your income, bank account details, or credit score.

Here are some specific steps you can take to protect your privacy on social media:

- Review your privacy settings and adjust them to limit who can see your posts and personal information. Consider making your accounts private so that only approved followers can see your content.
- Be cautious about accepting friend requests or follows from people you don't know in real life. Scammers often use fake profiles to try to gain access to personal information
- Avoid sharing sensitive personal information, such as your full birthdate, address, or phone number, on your public profiles.
- Be mindful of the photos and videos you share, and avoid posting anything that could reveal sensitive information, such as your location or financial status.
- Use strong, unique passwords for all of your social media accounts, and enable two-factor authentication whenever possible.

It's also important to be cautious about the information you share on other online platforms, such as online forums, comment sections, or personal websites. Avoid sharing sensitive personal or financial information in public spaces, and be mindful of the digital trail you leave behind.

Device Security

It's also important to secure your mobile devices, such as your smartphone or tablet, with strong passwords, fingerprint recognition, or facial recognition. These devices often contain a wealth of sensitive information, including financial data and login credentials, making them a prime target for thieves and hackers. By securing your devices with strong authentication measures, you can help prevent unauthorized access to your information.

Here are some additional tips for securing your mobile devices:

- Enable automatic software updates to ensure that your device is always running the latest security patches and features.
- Download apps only from trusted sources, such as the official app store for your device. Avoid downloading apps from third-party sites or links, as these may contain malware or other security threats.
- Be cautious about granting apps access to your location, contacts, or other sensitive information. Only allow access to apps that you trust and that have a legitimate need for the information.
- Use a secure password manager to help you generate and store strong, unique passwords for all of your

accounts, including those accessed on your mobile device.

- Enable remote wiping capabilities on your device, so that you can erase all of your personal information if your device is ever lost or stolen.

Defunct Device Disposal

Picture this: you're about to bid farewell to your trusty old laptop, the one that's been with you through thick and thin. It's served you well, but now it's time for an upgrade. So, you wipe a nostalgic tear from your eye, and prepare to send your digital companion off to greener pastures.

But wait! Before you hand over your beloved device to a stranger or toss it in the trash, there's something crucial you must do:

Ensure that all your personal information is securely erased from its memory banks.

Now, you might be tempted to simply drag all your files to the trash and call it a day. But hold on there, buckaroo! Just because you can't see those files anymore doesn't mean they're gone for good. With the right tools and a little bit of technical wizardry, a determined snoop could resurrect your deleted data faster than you can say "identity theft."

To truly protect your digital footprint, you'll need to take a more thorough approach. Enter data eraser tools. These powerful programs will scour every nook and cranny of your device, completely obliterating your personal information. Sounds extreme, but that's exactly what we want in this case.

But if you really want to satisfy your insatiable appetite for information destruction, you can take things a step further...

Imagine yourself in a dimly lit room, hunched over your old hard drive, cackling maniacally—power drill in hand. With a few well-placed holes through the platters, you'll render that drive more unreadable than a doctor's handwriting. It's the ultimate form of data destruction.

So, as you say goodbye to your old digital devices, remember: your personal information is a precious commodity. With a little bit of effort and the right tools, you can ensure that your digital footprint stays safe, secure, and out of the wrong hands.

ACTIVITY: Financial Security Checklist

Utilize this checklist to evaluate and enhance your financial security measures, ensuring the protection of your finances.

1. Conduct a Financial Audit:

- Review your bank, credit card, and investment statements for unauthorized transactions.
- Use budgeting apps to monitor spending and identify anomalies.
- Report any suspicious activities to your financial institutions immediately.

2. Secure Your Documents:

- Store physical financial documents in a fireproof safe.

- Maintain digital copies in encrypted storage like password-protected cloud services.
- Shred sensitive documents before disposal.
- Regularly back up important digital documents.

3. Protect Your Identity:

- Obtain and review your free credit reports annually.
- Enable two-factor authentication for online accounts.
- Use strong and unique passwords.

4. Stay Safe Online:

- Be wary of unsolicited requests for personal information.
- Verify sources before clicking links or downloading attachments.
- Conduct financial transactions over secure, private networks.
- Limit personal information shared on social media and online.

5. Secure Your Devices:

- Set strong passwords on all devices.
- Regularly update devices and apps with security patches.
- Install reputable antivirus software.
- Enable device location and remote wiping features for lost or stolen devices.
- Be selective about app permissions.

6. Dispose of Old Devices Securely:

- Use certified data eraser tools to wipe old devices.
- Physically destroy old storage devices to prevent data recovery. *Power drill, sledgehammer... I won't judge.*

Reminder: Financial security is an ongoing effort. Regularly update your security practices to address new threats. Stay proactive and vigilant to safeguard your financial future.

Chapter 10

Planning For Major Life Expenses

Savings only have meaning when you have a purpose for them. Plan for what's important.
—Robert Kiyosaki

As you navigate through life, you'll encounter a variety of significant financial milestones. These larger expenses can be daunting, especially if you're not prepared. But here's the good news: by anticipating them early on, you can set yourself up for success and achieve your goals without breaking the bank.

Saving for a First Car, College and Travel

One of the most important things you can do as a young person is to start saving and planning for the big expenses that come with adulthood. Whether it's buying your first car, paying for college, or taking that dream vacation, taking a smart financial approach can make all the difference.

Your First Car

When it comes to making your first car purchase as a teenager, it's essential to approach the decision with a mix of excitement and practicality. While it might be tempting to go for that shiny new sports car that's been catching your eye, a more prudent choice would be to opt for a reliable used vehicle.

Not only can a pre-owned car save you a considerable amount of money upfront, but it can also help you sidestep the rapid depreciation that new cars experience in their first few years. Think of it as letting someone else take the financial hit while you reap the benefits of a well-maintained, wallet-friendly ride.

Of course, before you start your car-buying adventure, it's crucial to consider the total cost of ownership beyond the sticker price. Insurance, maintenance, and fuel costs can pile up faster than your growing pile of laundry, so be sure to factor these expenses into your budget.

To get the best deal possible, put on your detective hat and do some thorough research. Compare prices from multiple dealerships and sellers, and don't be afraid to channel your inner negotiator. Remember, a little haggling can go a long way in saving you some hard-earned cash.

By making a smart, informed decision when buying your first car, you'll be setting yourself up for a smoother financial journey down the road. And who knows? You might even impress your friends with your savvy car-buying skills while they're still trying to figure out how to parallel park.

College-Bound

Another major expense you might encounter as a young adult is paying for higher education. Whether you're planning to attend a four-year university, community college, or vocational school, the cost of tuition, books, and living expenses can quickly add up. That's why it's important to start planning and saving for college as early as possible.

One popular option for college savings is a 529 plan. These tax-advantaged investment accounts allow you to save money specifically for education expenses, and many states offer additional tax benefits for contributions. Another option is a Coverdell Education Savings Account (ESA), which functions similarly to a 529 plan but with lower contribution limits and more flexibility in how the funds can be used.

When planning for college, it's also important to consider the impact of in-state versus out-of-state tuition. Attending a public university in your home state can often be significantly cheaper than going out of state or to a private school. However, if you have your heart set on a particular program or school, it may be worth the extra cost. The key is to weigh your options carefully and make an informed decision based on your goals and financial situation.

Travel

Finally, let's talk about travel. While it may not be as essential as transportation or education, exploring new places and cultures can be a truly life-enriching and perspective-enhancing experience. However, travel can also be expensive, especially if you're planning international trips or luxury getaways. That's why it's important to start saving for travel early and to be strategic about how you allocate your funds.

One effective strategy is to set specific travel goals and create a dedicated savings fund for each one. For example, if you're dreaming of backpacking through Europe after graduation, start setting aside a portion of your income each month into a separate account earmarked for that trip. You can also look for ways to save on travel expenses, such as booking flights and accommodations well in advance, traveling during off-peak seasons, and taking advantage of student discounts and loyalty programs.

By prioritizing your travel goals and being proactive about saving, you can turn your dream adventures abroad into a reality without breaking the bank.

Wedding Budgeting

For many young couples, diving into wedding planning can be their first plunge into deep financial waters together. Given that the average wedding in the United States can cost about as much as a brand-new car, it's no surprise that sticker shock can turn what should be a joyous occasion into a nail-biting budgetary circus. Trying to juggle the costs of venues, catering, and all those flowers *(why are there always so many flowers?)* can make even the calmest couples consider eloping.

Get Real

The first step to tackling the financial beast that is a wedding is to have a real heart-to-heart talk with your fiancé. Start by laying all your financial cards on the table — *and no bluffing!* This is where you figure out if your wedding budget is more about champagne and caviar or beer and pretzels.

Determine how much you can truly afford to save for the wedding without banking on winning the lottery in the meantime, and then allocate your funds with that number in mind. This approach helps ensure that your wedding plans are built on a foundation of financial sanity rather than whimsical thinking.

Focus Where It Matters Most

It's easy to fall into the trap of blowing half your budget on things like a designer dress that costs more than a downpayment on a house or floral arrangements that rival a botanical garden. Remember, while these things might make for stunning photos, they don't actually do much to enhance the overall enjoyment of your guests.

Instead, focus your financial firepower on the aspects of the wedding that genuinely matter and improve the experience— like ensuring the food is delicious, the band can actually play, and the photographer won't just take blurry selfies. These are the elements you'll actually remember—not the 500 custom, hand-embossed place cards.

Keep It Simple

Simplicity isn't just a style, it's a budgetary strategy. Think about hosting a smaller, more intimate gathering rather than a blockbuster wedding that might rival an awards show in logistics and cost. Perhaps choose a venue that's naturally beautiful, like a public park or a family backyard, where Mother Nature does most of the decorating for free.

Investing in some tasteful lighting and elegant decor can turn a simple space into a fairy-tale setting. This way, you can save on venue costs and splurge on things that enhance the ambiance without draining your bank account.

Avoid Financing

When it comes to paying for your wedding, it's important to approach the process with a clear head and a realistic budget. While it may be tempting to splash out on your big day, taking on significant debt to finance your nuptials can put a lasting strain on your new marriage and your long-term financial health.

Instead of relying on loans or credit cards to cover the cost of your wedding, consider saving up and paying for as much as possible out of pocket. This may mean making some tough choices and sacrifices in the short term, but it will pay off in the long run by allowing you to start your married life on a solid financial footing.

If you do receive contributions from family members, be sure to have an open and honest conversation about any expectations or strings attached to the money. It's important to make sure everyone is on the same page and that you're not feeling pressured to spend more than you're comfortable with.

Ultimately, the key to a successful and stress-free wedding is to focus on what really matters: celebrating your love and commitment to each other. By prioritizing your values and being mindful of your spending, you can create a meaningful and memorable day without breaking the bank or taking on unnecessary debt.

Homeownership Basics

For many people, buying a home is the biggest financial decision they'll ever make. It's a major milestone that can provide a sense of stability, security, and pride—but it's also a significant investment that requires careful planning and consideration.

Consider The "Hidden" Costs

We've talked about this before, but one of the first things to understand about homeownership is that it comes with a huge variety of costs beyond just the mortgage payment.

- **Utilities**: As a homeowner, you'll be responsible for paying all utility bills, including electricity, gas, water, sewer, and trash collection. These costs can vary greatly depending on the size of your home and your usage habits.
- **Property taxes**: You'll be responsible for paying annual property taxes based on the assessed value of your home. These taxes can vary widely depending on your location and are often used to fund local services like schools, libraries, and public safety.
- **Insurance**: Homeowners insurance is essential to protect your investment and provide financial security against unexpected events like property damage, theft, personal liability, and even natural events like flooding, tornados, and hurricanes.
- **HOA fees**: If you purchase a home within a community governed by a Homeowners' Association (HOA), you'll likely have to pay monthly or annual dues. These fees often cover the maintenance of common

areas, amenities, and sometimes even exterior upkeep of your home.

- **Landscaping and yard maintenance**: Keeping your lawn and garden in tip-top shape can be costly, especially if you need to hire professionals for tasks like mowing, trimming, and fertilizing.
- **Pest control**: Depending on where you live, you may need to budget for regular pest control services to keep critters like termites, ants, or rodents at bay.
- **Renovations and upgrades**: As a homeowner, you might want (or need) to update things like flooring, appliances, or fixtures over time. Even minor renovations can be expensive, so it's wise to set aside funds for these projects.
- **Furniture and decor**: Unless you're downsizing, you'll likely need to purchase additional furniture and decor to fill your new home. This can be a significant expense, especially if you have a larger space to furnish.
- **Emergency repairs**: Unfortunately, unexpected repairs like a leaky roof, burst pipe, or broken HVAC system can happen at any time. Having an emergency fund specifically for your home can help soften the blow of these surprise expenses.

By considering all of these potential costs, you'll be better equipped to create a comprehensive budget for homeownership. Remember, being prepared for these expenses can make the difference between a stressful and a successful homeowning experience!

Down Payment

Another key factor to consider is the down payment. In general, the larger your down payment, the lower your monthly mortgage payments will be. A larger down payment can also help you qualify for a better interest rate and avoid the need for private mortgage insurance (PMI). However, saving up for a substantial down payment can take time and discipline, especially if you're also juggling other financial priorities.

So, how much should you aim to save for a down payment? A good rule of thumb is to put down at least 20% of the purchase price. For example, if you're eyeing a home that costs $200,000, you'll want to have around $40,000 saved up. Now, I know what you might be thinking: *"I'll be as old as my grandparents by the time I save that much!"* But fear not, my friend. There are plenty of strategies you can use to speed up your savings, like automating your contributions, cutting back on unnecessary expenses, and exploring down payment assistance programs.

Of course, if you're struggling to come up with a 20% down payment, don't despair. You can still purchase a home with a smaller down payment, but be prepared to pay for Primary Mortgage Insurance (PMI), which is essentially an extra fee tacked onto your monthly mortgage payment to protect the lender in case you default.

At the end of the day, saving for a down payment takes patience, persistence, and a little bit of creativity. But trust me, when you're finally able to turn the key and step into your very own home, all that hard work will be worth it.

Mortgages

When it comes to choosing a mortgage, there are a few different options to consider. Fixed-rate mortgages offer predictable monthly payments over the life of the loan, while adjustable-rate mortgages (ARMs) may start with a lower interest rate but can fluctuate over time based on market conditions. There are also government-backed loan programs, such as FHA and VA loans, which can offer more flexible qualification requirements and lower down payment options for certain borrowers.

Ultimately, the type of mortgage that's right for you will depend on your individual financial situation and goals. It's important to do your research, compare rates and terms from multiple lenders, and choose a loan that aligns with your long-term financial plan.

Think Big Picture

When you're gearing up to shop for a home, it's crucial to keep your financial feet on the ground. Just because a bank might be willing to throw a mountain of money your way doesn't mean you should use it all to buy your dream castle. Remember, *the bank wants to load you up with debt for as long as possible*—because that means more money for them.

Sure, the idea of living in a home fit for royalty sounds great until you remember that castles come with royal upkeep costs too! Instead, take a good look at your income, debts, and how much you want to save for things like future vacations. Pick a home that fits your budget comfortably. Your bank account will thank you, and you'll still be able to afford your Netflix subscription.

Remember Maintenance

Ah, the delicate dance of budgeting for home maintenance—a tango where every move must be precise, every task foreseen, lest your hot water heater decides it's time for a spontaneous lunar vacation, oblivious to the roof in its path.

Let's say you have a humble abode valued at $100,000. Following the sage advice of financial gurus, you might want to earmark around 1% to 3% of that value annually for maintenance. That translates to roughly $83 to $250 a month, give or take, depending on the quirks and whims of your particular homestead.

Now, don't go digging behind the couch cushions for exact change just yet. Remember, this figure isn't set in stone; it's more like a compass pointing you in the general direction of financial preparedness. Some months, you might breeze through needing to replace only a lightbulb, while others might demand a bit more coin for unexpected surprises.

The key is to start with a solid estimate, stay nimble, and always keep a little extra in your back pocket for those inevitable *"home, sweet home"* moments.

Retirement Savings for Young Adults

When you're young and just starting out in your career, retirement can feel like a distant and abstract concept. After all, you have decades ahead of you to worry about saving for the future, right?

Well, not exactly. You've heard it before... *the earlier you start saving, the more time your money has to grow and compound over time.* In fact, thanks to the power of compound interest, even small contributions, especially early on, can have a significant impact on your retirement nest egg way down the line.

410K

So, how can you get started with retirement savings as a teen or young adult? One of the best options is to take advantage of employer-sponsored retirement plans, such as 401(k)s or pension plans. Many employers offer matching contributions, which means they'll match a certain percentage of the money you contribute to your retirement account. This is essentially free money that can help supercharge your savings over time.

If your employer doesn't offer a retirement plan or you're self-employed, you can also open an individual retirement account (IRA) on your own. There are two main types of IRAs: traditional and Roth. With a traditional IRA, you pay taxes when you retire. With a Roth IRA, you pay taxes before the money goes into the account.

I know that's getting into blah territory, so just remember this—when dealing with the whole "traditional" vs. "Roth" IRA thing, it really just depends on when you want to deal with taxes—now or later. For now, just remember that the most important thing is to start saving as early as possible so your money has plenty of time to grow!

Thinking Way (WAY) Ahead

The retirement conundrum—a perplexing puzzle where dreams of jet-setting clash with the allure of lazy afternoons with a good book. Do you envision sipping Mai Tais on a beach in Bora Bora, or do you imagine yourself being more of a *"binge-watch TV in your pajamas"* kind of retiree?

Whether you're plotting a lavish lifestyle filled with yachts and caviar or dreaming of cozy nights by the fireplace with loved ones and a faithful four-legged friend, your retirement savings plan needs to be as unique as you are. After all, there's no one-size-fits-all approach to funding your golden years. It's all about finding that perfect balance between living your best life and not having to shake your piggy bank upside down to make ends meet.

The 80% Rule

One helpful rule of thumb is the "80% rule," which suggests that you'll need to replace about 80% of your pre-retirement income to maintain your standard of living in retirement. So, if you're currently earning $50,000 per year, you'll need to have enough savings to generate about $40,000 per year in retirement.

Of course, this is just a rough estimate, and your actual retirement needs may vary based on a variety of factors, such as your health, life expectancy, and inflation rates. That's why it's important to work with a financial advisor or use online retirement calculators to create a personalized savings plan that takes into account your unique circumstances and goals.

The key is to start saving as early and as consistently as possible, even if you can only afford to contribute a small amount each month. Over time, those small contributions can add up to a significant nest egg that will provide you with financial security and freedom in your golden years.

Wrap-Up

At your age, it's easy to feel like the future is a distant, abstract concept and that you have all the time in the world to worry about things like buying a car, paying for college, planning a wedding, buying a home, and saving for retirement. However, the truth is that these significant financial milestones are headed your way a whole lot faster than you realize.

By taking the time to educate yourself about these upcoming expenses and the strategies you can use to manage them, you'll be able to navigate them predictably when it's time. With a little bit of foresight, planning, and discipline, you can manage these major financial milestones with confidence and set yourself up for a bright and secure future.

Activity: Life Expense Project

If you're ready to start planning for a major life expense, like buying a home, planning a wedding, or saving for retirement, this step-by-step activity will help you create a detailed and actionable plan. Let's get started!

Step 1—Choose your goal: Pick a major life expense that you want to start saving for. It could be something in the near future, like buying a car or paying for college, or a longer-term goal, like a down payment on a house or a dream vacation. Write down your chosen expense and make it specific.

Step 2—Research the costs: Once you have your goal in mind, it's time to do some research. Use online resources, such as real estate listings, wedding planning websites, or college cost calculators, to get a realistic estimate of how much money you'll need to save. Don't forget to factor in related expenses, like closing costs when buying a home or textbooks and supplies for college.

Step 3—Set a timeline: Now that you have a savings target in mind, break it down into smaller, more manageable milestones. Set realistic deadlines for each milestone based on your income, expenses, and other financial commitments. For example, if you're saving for a down payment on a house, you might aim to save $5,000 in the first year, $10,000 in the second year, and so on until you reach your goal.

Step 4—Identify potential obstacles: Life has a way of throwing curveballs when we least expect it. Take some time to brainstorm potential roadblocks or challenges that could impact your ability to save, such as unexpected expenses, changes in income, or competing financial priorities. Come up with strategies for overcoming these obstacles and staying on track with your savings plan.

Step 5—Create a budget: To turn your plan into action, you'll need a detailed budget that accounts for your income, expenses, and savings goals. Look for areas where you can cut back on discretionary spending, like dining out or subscription services, and redirect that money toward your savings. Consider boosting your income through side hustles, freelance work, or selling unwanted items. To make saving easier, set up automatic transfers from your checking account to a dedicated savings account each month.

Step 6—Track your progress: Staying motivated is key to achieving any long-term goal. Create a visual representation of your savings plan, such as a chart or graph, and update it regularly to track your progress. Celebrate each milestone along the way and use any setbacks as an opportunity to reassess and adjust your plan as needed.

By following these steps and staying committed to your goal, you'll have a huge head-start on planning for your major life expenses. Remember, the earlier you start saving and planning, the more time you'll have to reach your target and the less stress you'll feel along the way.

Chapter 11

Philanthropy and Financial Sharing

No one is useless in this world who lightens the burdens of another. —Charles Dickens

Philanthropy involves donating money, resources, or time to help make life better for other people. This practice isn't just about the impact you can make on the world—significant as that is—it also enriches your own life.

When you give your time, skills, or money to a cause you care about, you're not just helping others—you're also gaining a sense of purpose, connection, and fulfillment that can't be measured in dollars and cents.

The Importance of Giving Back

It's easy to get caught up in our own lives and struggles, especially when we're young and still figuring things out. But the truth is, we're all part of something much bigger than ourselves—a community, a society, a world that needs our help.

When we give back, we're not just making a difference in the lives of others—we're also strengthening the very fabric of our communities. Think about it: every time you volunteer at a local food bank, donate to a school fundraiser, or support a charity that provides clean water to families in need, you're helping to create a more compassionate and sustainable world for everyone.

Tithing

One approach to giving back is to commit to donating a percentage of your income, such as 10%, to causes you care about. This practice, known as tithing, has roots in various religious traditions but has been adopted by many as a way to make giving a regular habit.

By setting aside a portion of your income for tithing, you ensure that giving back remains a priority even as your financial situation changes. You can choose to donate your 10% to a single cause or spread it out among multiple organizations that align with your values.

Perspective Shift

The benefits of giving back go beyond just the tangible impact on others. Studies have shown that engaging in philanthropy and volunteering can actually boost our own well-being and happiness. When we focus on helping others, we shift our attention away from our own problems and gain a sense of perspective and gratitude. We also build connections with like-minded people and develop new skills and knowledge that can serve us well in other areas of our lives.

In fact, some experts believe that cultivating a habit of generosity and giving back can be one of the most powerful things we can do for our mental and emotional health. It's a way of tapping into our innate desire to be part of something larger than ourselves and to use our unique gifts and talents to make a difference in the world.

The Ripple Effect

Of course, giving back doesn't have to mean donating large sums of money or dedicating all your free time to volunteering. Even small acts of kindness and generosity can have a ripple effect, inspiring others to pay it forward and creating a culture of compassion and mutual support.

Imagine if everyone in your community committed to doing one small act of kindness or generosity each day. Whether it's helping a neighbor with their groceries, donating a few dollars to a local charity, or simply offering a smile and a kind word to someone who looks like they could use it. Over time, those small actions would add up to a tidal wave of positive change, transforming your community from the inside out.

So, as you navigate your own financial journey, don't forget to make room for giving back. Whether it's through volunteering your time, donating your money, or simply spreading kindness and compassion wherever you go, every act of generosity matters—and it all starts with you.

Finding Causes You Care About

Now that we've established why giving back is so important, let's talk about how to get started. One of the biggest challenges many people face when it comes to philanthropy is figuring out where to direct their time, energy, and resources. With so many worthy causes and organizations out there, it can be overwhelming to know where to begin.

The Big Questions

That's why the first step in any philanthropic journey is to identify the causes and issues that truly resonate with you.

- What are the problems in the world that keep you up at night?
- What are the injustices that make your blood boil?
- What are the dreams and aspirations you have for your community, your country, or the planet as a whole?

These are the questions that can help guide you toward the causes and organizations that align with your deepest values and passions. Because when you're working on something that truly matters to you, it doesn't feel like work at all. It feels like a calling, a purpose, a way of making your mark on the world.

What's Important To You - and Why?

One way to start identifying your philanthropic priorities is to take some time for self-reflection and exploration. Write down a list of the issues and causes that you care about most, and think about why they matter to you.

- Maybe you're passionate about protecting the environment because you grew up near a beautiful natural area that's now under threat from development.

- Maybe you're committed to fighting poverty because you've seen firsthand how lack of access to education and opportunity can hold people back.
- Maybe you're dedicated to supporting the arts because you believe in the power of creativity and self-expression to transform lives and communities.

Whatever your reasons, take the time to really understand what drives you and what you want to achieve through your philanthropic efforts. This will help you narrow down your focus and find organizations and initiatives that align with your goals and values.

Once you have a sense of what matters most to you, it's time to start researching potential charities and non-profit organizations to support. This is where due diligence comes in—because not all charitable organizations are created equal, and it's important to make sure your hard-earned money and time are going to reputable, effective, and transparent groups.

Navigating Charities

One excellent resource for researching charities is Charity Navigator, a website that provides detailed ratings and information on thousands of non-profit organizations. You can search for charities by cause, location, or rating, and get a clear picture of their financial health, accountability, and transparency.

Other helpful resources include GuideStar, which provides in-depth financial and programmatic data on non-profits, and the Better Business Bureau's Wise Giving Alliance, which sets standards for charitable accountability and evaluates organizations based on those criteria.

When researching potential charities to support, it's important to look beyond just the surface-level marketing and branding. Take the time to read through their mission statements, annual reports, and financial statements to get a sense of how they operate and what kind of impact they're having.

Look for organizations with a clear track record of success, a commitment to transparency and accountability, and a focus on long-term, sustainable change rather than short-term band-aid solutions.

Local, National, or Global

It's also worth considering whether you want to focus your philanthropic efforts on local, national, or global causes. Each level of impact has its own unique challenges and opportunities, and there's no one-size-fits-all answer.

Some people prefer to support local organizations that are making a difference in their own backyard. In contrast, others are drawn to global initiatives that address systemic issues on a broader scale. Ultimately, the key is to find a balance that feels right for you and aligns with your personal values and priorities.

Remember, finding causes you care about is an ongoing process. Your priorities and interests may shift over time as you learn and grow. But by starting with a clear sense of what matters most to you and doing your due diligence to find reputable organizations to support, you'll be well on your way to making a meaningful impact through your philanthropic efforts.

CAUTION: Not All Causes Are Noble

In today's world of social media and instant information, it's easy to get caught up in the hype surrounding various causes and movements. However, not all causes are created equal, and some even have hidden agendas and misinformation at their core.

These shameful causes heavily rely on people being uninformed and fueled by strong emotions, such as anger, fear, or a sense of injustice. They may use inflammatory language or sensationalized stories to provoke an emotional response rather than presenting a balanced and factual perspective. By preying on people's emotions and lack of knowledge, these causes can quickly gain traction and support, even if their underlying goals or methods are twisted and harmful.

One of the first steps in educating yourself on the true purpose of the cause, charity, or movement is to look beyond the surface-level messaging and dig deeper into the facts and data behind the scenes. Be wary of sources that seem to push a particular agenda or that rely heavily on anecdotal evidence rather than hard facts.

Ask yourself:

- Who stands to benefit from this cause?
- Is this cause built on a foundation of love or hate?
- Is it's purpose to tear people down or build them up?
- Are there any hidden political or financial interests at play?
- Are the leaders transparent about their goals?

By critically examining the underlying factors behind a cause, you can better assess whether it aligns with your own values and priorities.

Another key aspect of educating yourself is to seek out diverse perspectives and engage in open-minded dialogue with others. Don't just surround yourself with people who already agree with you. Actively seek out differing viewpoints and be willing to listen and learn from those who may challenge your assumptions. This can help you gain a more nuanced and well-rounded understanding of complex issues, and can also help you identify potential red flags or areas of concern.

Ultimately, the key to avoiding false causes is to approach philanthropy and activism with a critical and discerning eye. Don't just follow the crowd or jump on the latest bandwagon. Take the time to educate yourself, ask tough questions, and make informed decisions based on facts and evidence. By doing so, you can ensure that your efforts to make a difference in the world are truly meaningful, effective, and positive.

Volunteering Your Time

While donating money to charitable causes is undoubtedly important, it's not the only way to make a difference in the world. In fact, one of the most potent forms of philanthropy is volunteering your time and skills to support the causes you care about.

Volunteering offers a unique opportunity to get hands-on with the issues and organizations you're passionate about and to see the impact of your efforts firsthand. Whether you're tutoring kids at a local school, helping out at a community garden, or using your professional skills to support a non-profit's mission, volunteering allows you to be an active participant in creating positive change.

Skill-Based Volunteering

One particularly impactful way to volunteer is through skills-based volunteering, where you use your unique expertise and experience to support a charitable organization's work.

For example, if you're a graphic designer, you could volunteer to create marketing materials for a local non-profit. If you're a web developer, you could help build a website for a grassroots advocacy group. If you're a writer, you could contribute content to a charity's blog or newsletter.

Skills-based volunteering not only allows you to make a tangible difference in the work of a charitable organization, but it also offers a chance to build your skills and experience in a meaningful way. It's a win-win situation. You get to give back to a cause you care about while also sharpening your own skillset along the way.

Making Connections

Another benefit of volunteering is the opportunity to build connections with like-minded individuals and organizations. When you volunteer, you're joining a community of people who share your passion for making a difference in the world. You'll meet new friends, learn from experienced activists and leaders, and become part of a network of changemakers who support and inspire each other.

These connections can be particularly valuable for young people who are just starting out in their careers or exploring their personal and professional interests. Volunteering can open doors to new opportunities, mentorship relationships, and even job prospects down the line. It's a way of building social capital and expanding your horizons in a way that feels authentic and aligned with your values.

The Role of Youth in Philanthropy

When it comes to philanthropy and financial sharing, young people have a particularly unique and powerful role to play. As the leaders of tomorrow, you have the energy, creativity, and vision to drive social change and build a better world for everyone.

Fresh Perspectives

One of the key ways that young people can make a difference through philanthropy is by bringing fresh perspectives and new ideas to the table. Because youth are often less constrained by traditional ways of thinking and doing things, they're able to approach problems with a sense of curiosity, experimentation, and innovation. They're not afraid to challenge the status quo or to imagine bold new solutions to complex challenges.

This kind of outside-the-box thinking is precisely what's needed to tackle some of the most significant issues facing our world today. From environmental issues to social inequality to healthcare access to educational disparities. By bringing your unique perspective and skills to bear on these challenges, you have the potential to create real, lasting change.

Advocating For Change

Another way that youth can make a difference through philanthropy is by serving as powerful advocates and change agents within their communities. Because young people are often deeply connected to the issues and challenges facing their peers and neighbors, they're uniquely positioned to raise awareness, mobilize support, and drive grassroots action.

For example, imagine a group of high school students who are passionate about reducing food waste and hunger in their community. They could start by organizing a food drive at their school, collecting surplus food from local businesses and farms, and distributing it to families in need. They could also advocate for policy changes at the local level, such as incentives for businesses to donate excess food or funding for school meal programs.

By taking action and speaking out on the issues that matter most to them, young people can inspire others to get involved and create a ripple effect of positive change. They can also build valuable leadership skills and gain a sense of empowerment and agency in shaping the world around them.

Barriers For Participation

Of course, getting involved in philanthropy and financial sharing as a young person isn't always easy. Many youth face barriers to participation, such as lack of access to resources, limited time and energy, or skepticism from adults who may not take their ideas and contributions seriously.

That's why it's so important for adults—whether they're parents, teachers, mentors, or community leaders—to support and empower young people in their philanthropic efforts. This can mean providing resources and guidance, connecting youth with like-minded organizations and individuals, or simply listening to their ideas and taking them seriously.

It's also important for young people themselves to seek out opportunities for education and leadership development in the philanthropic space. This can include attending workshops and conferences, joining youth-led organizations and networks, or seeking out mentorship from experienced activists and changemakers.

Connected Community

By investing in their own learning and growth, young people can build the skills, knowledge, and confidence they need to be effective advocates and leaders in the philanthropic world. They can also connect with a community of peers who share their passion for making a difference and who can offer support, inspiration, and accountability along the way.

Ultimately, the role of youth in philanthropy is about recognizing the incredible potential and power that young people have to create positive change in the world. By empowering and supporting youth to get involved in charitable giving and volunteering, we're not only making a difference in the lives of others—we're also investing in the future leaders and changemakers who will shape our world for generations to come.

Activity: Charity Research Project

Enhance your understanding of philanthropy and discover how you can contribute to causes you care about.

Step 1: Identify Your Interests

Write down three issues or causes that you are passionate about. These could range from environmental conservation to supporting education for underprivileged children.

Step 2: Research

Choose one cause from your list. Use the internet to find three charities that work in this area. Look for information on their missions, the work they do, and their impact.

Step 3: Evaluate Credibility

For each charity, check their transparency and credibility. Use resources like Charity Navigator, GuideStar, or the Better Business Bureau to see ratings and reviews.

Step 4: Interview or Visit

If possible, arrange a visit or a virtual meeting with a representative from one of the charities. Prepare at least five questions about how they use donations, their significant projects, and how volunteers can get involved.

Step 5: Reflect

Write a one-page reflection on what you learned. Include:

- Why the cause is important to you?
- Which charity did you feel most aligned with and why?

- How can you see yourself contributing to the cause in the future, either through donations, volunteering, or raising awareness?

By completing this project, you will gain a better understanding of how charitable organizations operate and the significant impact your contributions can make. You'll also develop skills in research, critical thinking, and effective communication.

Chapter 12
Conclusion

First off, a ***HUGE congratulations*** to you!

You've made it to the end of our journey together through the world of personal finance. You've learned practical tips and strategies for managing your money, as well as the mindset and habits that can set you up for long-term financial success.

But more than that, ***you've taken a measurable step towards financial literacy and empowerment***. By dedicating your time and attention to this book, you've shown a commitment to understanding and taking control of your future.

By sharing your thoughts and experiences, you can inspire and guide other teens who are just starting their own financial journeys.

The best way to make an impact is by leaving a review of this book on Amazon. Leave your review by scanning the QR code:

Your honest feedback will not only help other readers discover the value of this book but also encourage them to start their own path toward financial literacy and empowerment.

Thank you for choosing to invest in yourself and your financial future.

Thank you for giving me the opportunity to share my knowledge and insights with you.

Thank you for being a part of a growing movement of young people who are taking control of their financial lives and blazing a trail toward a brighter tomorrow.

So, here's to you, my money-savvy friend. May your financial journey be filled with endless opportunities, rewarding challenges, and the satisfaction of knowing that you're creating a life of abundance, security, and joy.

Keep learning, keep growing, and most of all, keep believing in yourself and your limitless potential.

With gratitude and admiration,

Conclusion

Ben Clardy

www.ingramcontent.com/pod-product-compliance
Lightning Source LLC
Chambersburg PA
CBHW071408120626
46546CB00002B/861